SPIRITUALITY AND LIBERATION

Robert McAfee Brown

SPIRITUALITY AND LIBERATION

Overcoming the Great Fallacy

First published in Great Britain 1988

Spire is an imprint of Hodder & Stoughton *Publishers*

Some scripture quotations are the author's own paraphrases.

British Library Cataloguing in Publication Data

Brown, Robert McAfee, *1920–*
Spirituality and liberation.
1. Christian life. Spirituality
I. Title
248.4

ISBN 0-340-48930-8

First published in the USA by
The Westminster Press, Philadelphia.

Printed in Great Britain for Hodder and Stoughton Limited, Mill Road, Dunton Green, Sevenoaks, Kent by Richard Clay Limited, Bungay, Suffolk. Photoset by Rowland Phototypesetting Limited, Bury St Edmunds, Suffolk.

Hodder and Stoughton Editorial Office: 47 Bedford Square, London WC1B 3DP.

Theology is not a provable accumulation,
like science, nor is it a succession
of enduring monuments, like art.
It must always unravel and be reknit.

John Updike, *Hugging the Shore*

Contents

PART II Clues for Construction

PART III Radical Reconstruction

Acknowledgments

This book, several years in the making, creates indebtedness to many people. I must thank some of them, while simultaneously absolving them of responsibility for shortcomings that slipped through the cracks.

Among individuals, special thanks to my sons Peter and Mark, who took the photographs that are discussed in the Transition after Chapter 3, with the hope that more and more of their artistic vision will rub off on me; to Sydney, whose gentle and firm attempts for forty-five years to keep me theologically honest ("Do you really mean that?") account for whatever integrity the text possesses; to Denise and John Carmody, Jim and Wilys Claire Nelson, Donald Gelpi, SJ, Karen Lebacqz, and Janet Walton, who have all made special contributions to my understanding of spirituality and liberation; to Judy Dunbar, who demonstrated that "friend" and "critic" are not mutually exclusive terms; to Elie Wiesel, whose commitment to liberation for all people has a hardly won spirituality within it, whether he would call it that or not; to Sr Joan Delaplane, OP, for a quotation from Augustine (used to begin Chapter 10) that has empowered me ever since I heard her use it; to members of the Religion Department at Carleton College, valued colleagues while the manuscript was being revised, and especially to Professor Anne Patrick, without whose counsel (and typewriter) the book would still be languishing; to Leslie Argueta-Vogel, living in El Salvador, for many third world materials; and, in ways beyond all telling of them, to Gustavo Gutiérrez, whose influence will be noticeable at every crucial point in the argument.

I owe special thanks to students in a class in the Network Programme of the Graduate Theological Union, in which we developed a course on "Prayer and Social Justice"; to Professor Bernard Adeney of New College, Berkeley, with whom I team-taught a course at the Graduate Theological Union on "Spirituality and Justice", and to Sr Clare Ronzani, SND, for opportunities to explore portions of the material with participants in the Institute for Spirituality and Worship at the Jesuit School of Theology.

Four books were especially helpful during the actual time of writing: Walter Brueggemann, Sharon Parks, and Thomas Groome's *To Act Justly, Love Tenderly, Walk Humbly*; Donal Dorr, *Spirituality and Justice*; Elizabeth O'Connor, *Journey Inward, Journey Outward*; and Roger Haight, *An Alternative Vision*.

Material from these pages formed the basis for the Snuggs Lectures at the University of Tulsa, Tulsa, Oklahoma; for the Ecumenical Chair in Theology Lecture series at Xavier University, Cincinnati, Ohio; and for talks at the Hennepin Avenue Methodist Church, Minneapolis, Minnesota, and the Lutheran Theological Seminary in Philadelphia. I benefited greatly from the discussion elicited on each of these occasions.

Most of the material appears in print for the first time, with the exception of a few pages and paragraphs from my chapter in Lee Cormie and Richard Snyder, eds, *Theology and the Struggle for Liberation: responses from the mainstream* (Maryknoll, NY, Orbis Books, 1988), and articles on "Spirituality and Liberation" published in the *Sewanee University Journal of Theology* and *Worship* (published at St John's Abbey in Minnesota), and, as "Espiritualidad y liberación" in *Vida y Reflexión* (Lima, Peru), 1983. A few of the comments on Henri Nouwen first appeared in *National Catholic Reporter*.

ROBERT MCAFEE BROWN

Northfield, Minnesota

Introduction

an episode, a few distinctions and some clarifications

Prayer is not the first thing that a person does. Before praying one experiences an existential shock.

Leonardo Boff, *The Lord's Prayer*

To clasp hands in prayer is the beginning of an uprising against the disorder of the world.

Karl Barth

[I have been learning] a beautiful and harsh truth, that the Christian faith does not separate us from the world but immerses us in it; that the church, therefore, is not a fortress set apart from the city, but a follower of the Jesus who loved, worked, struggled, and died in the midst of the city.

Archbishop Oscar Romero, shortly before he was shot for interfering with life "in the midst of the city"

June 16, 1985 started out like any other Sunday. Children were scrubbed and prepared for Sunday school, choirs got together early to practise the morning anthem, ministers looked over their manuscripts, wishing they had devoted more time to sermon preparation. And in many churches that day, when eleven o'clock finally rolled around, the pastors, acknowledging that these are troubled times and that in troubled times people are in special need of God's help, read a statement that had been circulated to the churches throughout the nation, entitled "A Theological Rationale and a Call to Prayer . . ." urging a renewed dedication to devotional life, all preceded by a biblical and historical "rationale", complete with fourteen footnotes.

Ho-hum.

The pious could be pleased that the church was once again attending to its "real job". Church officials could feel encouraged that their denominations were rallying together under the banner of prayer. And government officials could breathe more easily, now that the churches were "looking inward" once again, rather than messing around with politics and social action.

But it didn't work out that way. All the expectations were dashed. The pious were greatly agitated, upset that prayer had been used for partisan political ends. Church officials were deeply divided, some describing the "Call" as "presumptuous" and others as "contrary to scripture and tradition". And government officials were apoplectic, furiously charging that the church had intruded into areas where it didn't belong, engaging in what amounted to acts of treason. Prayer as an act of treason. The newspapers were full of it for weeks.

All this furore simply over a call to prayer? What could be more appropriate than for churches to commend a deeper prayer life to their constituents?

But the furore was real. For the country was South Africa; the date was the anniversary of the Soweto uprising of June 16, 1976, when government troops had entered this black township of Johannesburg and opened fire on black children; and the full title of "A Theological Rationale and a Call to Prayer . . ." was "A Theological Rationale and a Call to Prayer *for the End to Unjust Rule.*" Excerpts:

> We now pray that God will replace the present unjust structures of oppression with ones that are just, and remove from power those who persist in defying his laws, installing

> in their places leaders who will govern with justice and mercy . . .
>
> The present regime, together with its structures of domination, stands in contradiction to the Christian gospel to which the churches of the land seek to remain faithful . . .
>
> We pray that God in his grace may remove from his people the tyrannical structures of oppression and the present rulers in our country who persistently refuse to hear the cry for justice . . .
>
> We pledge ourselves to work for that day. (Cited in Allan A. Boesak and Charles Villa-Vicencio, eds, *When Prayer Makes News* (Westminster Press, 1986), pp. 26, 29.)

Strong meat.

The "Call to Prayer" was not blanketed with smooth generalities or bland exhortations. It stated without equivocation that the situation in South Africa was an offence to God and consequently an offence to God's people, that the present government was responsible for this offensive state of affairs, and that its leaders must therefore be replaced by new leaders committed to "justice and mercy". It not only pleaded with God to bring these changes about, it served notice to God and the state that those who offered the prayers were not going to leave it to God alone but were themselves pledged "to work for that day". No wonder that the published report of these events was entitled *When Prayer Makes News*.

Should prayer "make news"? Is it the job of church people to pray for the overthrow of their government? Does religion have anything to do with politics? Can one's private faith in God be enlisted as a vehicle for changing public policy? Were those church folk right to propose a change of government within a service of worship? Aren't "spiritual" matters (like prayer) and "liberation" matters (like politics) meant to be kept separate?

It is questions such as these, particularly the last, that are addressed in this book.

The questions are not new. They have been front and centre ever since Pharaoh unsuccessfully tried to persuade Moses that religion had nothing to do with Egypt's domestic policy on the status of nonindentured servants. God rather aggressively got into the act on Moses' side, and Pharaoh wound up a distant second in a field of two.

The structure of the argument should be clear from the contents and from the brief introduction to each of the three parts. Instead of repeating it again, let us reposition the question by brief comments on the two chief words of the title.

The book intends to offer an alternative to ongoing attempts to compartmentalize life into, roughly, the "sacred" and the "secular" (the former being "good" and the latter "evil"). One can ask why the terms "spirituality" and "liberation" were chosen to carry the weight of the argument. The answer is unedifyingly simple: These are the words most frequently used in current discussion, and they are usually invoked in such a way as to suggest that they are mutually exclusive. One can be "into spirituality", as many people have always been, or "into liberation", as increasing numbers of people appear to be. But that one could be "into" both, or that the dichotomy itself is suspect, are not notions that are entertained with generous affection.

In Latin America, Asia and Africa there are millions of people who once assumed that they were trapped in unfortunate situations with no option but to accept their lot and hope for a better deal after death. But a dream of liberation from all kinds of oppression, especially political and economic, has seized them and become the guiding star in their firmament. Things can be different, here and now.

The impulse is not only nurtured abroad. Within the United States a self-conscious embrace of the liberation message has empowered blacks to work for freedom from the various bondages imposed on them, and the same has been true of liberation movements in the lives of women, native Americans, gays, lesbians, Asian-Americans and a host of others.

Many of these liberation movements have arisen in, or been nurtured by, the church, and in all parts of the world "liberation theologies" have appeared, to provide religious grounding for the struggle.

In the commonly held understanding, liberation is pursued chiefly to establish a new social order that will wipe out the oppressive structures to which disadvantaged people have been subjected and create a society where all, and not just some, can live creative lives.

Similarly there are millions of people with a vision described by the word "spirituality". They do not necessarily look on political and economic structures as unimportant, but they do not see them as primary vehicles of redemption. For them, spirituality is a state of being, frequently approached through "spiritual exercises" and acts of discipline that put them in touch with realities, or a Reality, not discernible in ordinary experience. Deepening a relation to that Reality is what life is all about.

This is not a new movement in the way that widespread concern for liberation is a new movement. Nor is it found chiefly or exclusively within "western religions", in the way that many liberation movements are prominently identified with Christianity. Much of the wisdom about a life of spirituality has been nurtured in Buddhist and Hindu settings, as well as in the mystical traditions of Judaism and Sufi Islam.

It is significant that within our own upwardly mobile and success-oriented culture, the appeal of such a spirituality is on the rise. Finding no lasting fulfilment in the rat race of modern capitalist society, many outwardly successful people seek ways to overcome the competitive pressure and attain a measure of serenity that will fill the emptiness and counter-balance the chaos that appears eager to destroy them.

These descriptions (which will need not only fine-tuning but considerable overhaul as we proceed) suggest two impulses of the human spirit so apparently foreign to each other as to reinforce our earlier suggestion that they are mutually exclusive. This is certainly how many of their proponents see them, and much of the difficulty of relating them is attributable to their deeply ingrained suspicion of each other. It will be the purpose of this book not simply to dispel some of those suspicions but, finally, to suggest a different approach altogether.

It remains only to clarify three sources of possible misunderstanding.

First of all these pages are not a how-to manual for the practice of either spirituality or liberation. They should not be consulted in the hope of finding techniques for approaching Reality in zones of quiet or for rebuilding the earth in the name of justice. There are plenty of books that do both, and some are listed in the bibliography. The aim is more modest. It is to provide an approach through which spirituality and liberation can begin to be seen as two ways of talking about the same thing, so that there is no necessity, or even a possibility, of making a choice between them.

My personal story has led me along the route of liberation concerns that I increasingly perceive as including all that spirituality truly means, a route that is undoubtedly reflected in the way the argument develops. But others may come to that identical conclusion from the opposite starting point. Let not such persons feel slighted in these pages; let them write their own accounts for the edification of us all.

If the theme of the book seems obvious, or its development laborious, I can only congratulate the reader for having escaped a debate that seems to flourish with renewed vigour every few years, as those who want to keep the dichotomy alive mount their battle stations once again. This book is only one in a long chain of efforts to reclaim territory unjustly seized.

Secondly I want to anticipate another possible misunderstanding. It will soon be clear that the *bête noire* of these pages is dualism, or dividing the world into two separate compartments, and that my concern is to deny the legitimacy of such division. In making my case, however, I may sometimes appear guilty of excessive authorial zeal by following too exclusively what the writer Charles Williams called the way of "the affirmation of images", according to which every created thing partially reveals God and can lead to God, human love being the most obvious example. But according to Williams, who exemplified this approach in most of his writing, there is another way, called "the negation of images", that reminds us how paltry are the insights we can derive from images in a fallen world, and how unreliable are any conclusions reached in that way. Adherents of such a position usually feel confident only to say what God is not, since positive images become idols and do not sufficiently acknowledge the remaining unlikenesses. It was Williams's contention that we must practise both ways, since each protects against the excesses of the other. The way of affirmation makes certain claims possible; the way of negation safeguards against claiming too much for the claims. While human love is a pointer to God's love, for example, it is not the same as God's love, and there are many things done in the name of human love that it would be manifestly wrong to offer as analogies to God's love. The unlikenesses must not be glossed over. Let the principle be invoked by the reader whenever the author is observed transgressing it.

Thirdly, while this is manifestly a book written by a Christian, it is not written solely for Christians. It is written for all people who are concerned about its subject matter, and especially those on whom the Christian tradition is most dependent, the Jews. Whenever possible, and especially at points that seem to separate Christians and Jews from one another, I have tried to indicate points of contact and sharing. What I have tried *not* to do is mute my own perspective, since that only fuzzes the issue. When there is a Christian insight to be made I try to make it, aware that for those moments at least the interest of others may wane (though I hope they might at least be curious). My own *rebbe*, Elie Wiesel, says that the more clearly he writes as a Jew, the more clearly he communicates to non-Jews, and my experience in reading him confirms that this is one of the secrets of his communicative power. The posture I adopt here tries to be a mirror image of his, save that by comparison my glass is cracked and tarnished. But I will be happy if I can succeed one tenth as well as he does, in building bridges between our two communities.

PART I

Deconstruction

WHEREIN *an effort is made to clear the decks so that a new proposal can be launched*

WHEREIN *it is shown that the Great Fallacy (long though it has flourished and impressive though its credentials may be) errs in dividing life into two separate compartments*

WHEREIN *it is further shown that previous attempts to overcome this separation likewise err, either by demolishing one of the partners in the discussion or attempting (with initial attractiveness) to synthesize them*

WHEREIN *it is next proposed that the imagery of "withdrawal and return", while appearing to reinforce the Great Fallacy, creates a threshold for approaching life in a more unified way*

AND WHEREIN *finally, by employing the insights of two photographs, a transition is provided to more constructive efforts in Part II*

1

The Great Fallacy: variations on a single theme

The body is the prisonhouse of the soul.
Many Greek philosophers
before Aristotle

The spiritual regimen that emerged from an essentially dualistic definition of human nature was a simple one: things were bad; the body was bad; suffering was good. If-it-hurts-it-must-be-holy became the standard of all activity.
Sr Joan Chittister, OSB,
describing the earlier mentality of the church

The subject matter of this book is not the Great Fallacy. But its proper subject cannot be attended to until the theme of the Great Fallacy has been examined. Just when we think we have pushed it out of the front door of our minds, it sneaks in the back door, all the more powerful for being more subtle. It is a formidable foe, present in many forms and variations.

Variations first, theme later

Let us consider some of the variations, as a way of approaching the theme.

IRATE PROTESTANT LAYPERSON: Pastor, you've got no right to bring the election into the pulpit. It's not your job to deal with political issues. Just remember, religion and politics don't mix.

IRATE CATHOLIC LAYPERSON: What are those bishops up to anyway? First they write a pastoral letter on nuclear weapons, and now they've done one on the economy. If they're so keen on writing pastoral letters, why don't they do one on prayer?

HARASSED PARISHIONER: I have enough of a problem simply getting through a week at the office. I don't come to church to be reminded of still more problems; I come to church to be reinforced for next week. If I want to hear about conditions in Central America I'll go to a rally.

CALM PARISHIONER: We all had a truly spiritual experience being off in the woods on retreat, far away from all the mess of the world we live in most of the time. For the first time in months, I felt really close to God.

ACTIVIST PASTOR: Our government is doing such terrible things in Nicaragua that I can hardly bear to train Sunday school teachers, call on the elderly, and conduct worship. Instead of singing hymns we ought to be sitting in at the Senator's office.

TROUBLED TEENAGER: I've got problems. What do I do about drugs? Is sex okay? How am I going to get a job when I get out of high school? I'm tired of getting dragged to church to sing boring hymns and pray to God.

TROUBLED TEENAGER: I've got a problem. How can I believe in God when there's so much evil in the world? That really bothers me. Can't God stop it? But the only thing the youth group wants to do is plan ski weekends.

IDEALIST PHILOSOPHER: God is Eternal Being, unchanging and therefore unaffected by what happens to us. If we want to enter the realm of Eternal Being, we have to clear our minds of earthly distractions and seek God through detachment.

IDEALISTIC REVOLUTIONARY: The only God I can believe in is one who helps us get the supplies we need to bring down our tyrannical government and set up an era of peace and justice for everyone.

THEOLOGIAN (who just might be an old-style Lutheran): The church's task is to initiate us into the spiritual kingdom where we can find salvation. God has decreed that politicians and businessmen and soldiers should run the earthly kingdom. As long as they don't interfere with our kingdom, we won't interfere with theirs.

All these variations point to a single theme: Life is divided into two areas, two spheres, two compartments, and if we know what's good for us we'll keep it that way.

What are these two areas? The words we use to describe them are legion. Here is a sampling, with space for still more:

A handy checklist of opposites we encounter in the real world (in no particular order)

sacred vs. secular
prayer vs. politics
faith vs. works
withdrawal vs. engagement
church vs. world
eternity vs. time
theory vs. practice
religion vs. ethics
soul vs. body
personal vs. social
spirit vs. flesh
holy vs. profane
heaven vs. earth
otherworldly vs. this-worldly
divine vs. human
meditation vs. agitation
mysticism vs. humanism
saint vs. sinner
spiritual vs. material
contemplation vs. action
God vs. humanity
inner vs. outer
love vs. justice
creeds vs. deeds
priest vs. prophet
evangelism vs. social action
abstinence vs. sex
immortality vs. resurrection

Greek vs. Hebrew
"verticalism" vs. "horizontalism"
transcendence vs. immanence
liturgy vs. legislation
Jesus the Christ vs. Jesus of Nazareth
theonomy vs. autonomy
spirituality vs. liberation
______________ vs. ______________
______________ vs. ______________
______________ vs. ______________
______________ vs. ______________

All of us identify some of these items. We know there is a difference between saint and sinner, prayer and politics, faith and works, and a few others. Some of us can't identify all of the terms. Unless we have gone to seminary we have not lost much sleep worrying about the differences between theonomy and autonomy or verticalism and horizontalism.

Not to worry. One virtue of the list is that if we can identify even a few of the polarities, we have already got the point: whatever words we use, we keep dividing life into two realms.

Some of the separations seem valid even if others do not. This is because they are deeply grounded in our cultural as well as our religious life. We use terms like "soul" and "body" all the time, for example, even if we're not quite sure what they mean, and we're bombarded with the notion that there are important distinctions between the "things of the spirit" (whatever they are) and the "things of the flesh" (with which we have detailed acquaintance).

It is the contention of this book – to be up-front about it from the very start – that these separations are not only awkward, inaccurate and unhelpful but that they are, in almost all cases, just plain wrong. They do not add meaning to our lives or give us good interpretive tools; on the contrary they distort our lives and lead us to faulty understandings of who we are and what the world is like. That is why the attempt to insist on such divisions is called the

Great Fallacy. A fallacy is not just a trifling error; it is a huge deception.

The Great Fallacy is nothing new

The Great Fallacy has been around a long time, despite the fact that Judaism, out of which Christianity grew, was never seduced by it. On the contrary Judaism has always had a positive view of the importance and sacredness of the created order and all who inhabit it. Indeed one of the most robust resources for Christianity in combating the Great Fallacy is deeper immersion in its Jewish roots.

One problem for the early Christians was that they found themselves living not in a predominantly Jewish culture but in a culture that was dominated by a Greek worldview. To get a hearing in the Greek culture they had to employ Greek terms and employ a Greek way of thinking. And for many Greeks of that time the Great Fallacy was the Great Truth. They believed that the body was evil and the soul good, that time was corrupt and eternity pure, that earth was to be shunned and heaven sought, that flesh was the seat of impurity and spirit the seat of blessedness.

To be "saved", in this kind of situation, was to disengage from the evil world. The message was clear: scorn the body for the sake of the soul, forsake earth for the sake of heaven, stamp out the flesh for the sake of blessedness.

At two crucial points the church resisted this message. It rejected a view known as Docetism (from the Greek *dokeo*, meaning "to seem or appear to be"), which argued that Jesus only "seemed" to be human, since pure Deity could not dwell in impure flesh; and it also rejected a more complicated position known as Gnosticism, which held that salvation could come only from "inside" information or wisdom (*gnosis*) that was discovered by turning one's back on the world.

Nevertheless, as Christianity developed and spread, the

temptation to cut the Christian cloth to fit the Greek pattern proved almost irresistible. The Desert Fathers and other monastics, for example, retreated from the world and its blandishments, feeling that only in isolated places could God be truly found; and Jesus, who had first been known as a very flesh-and-blood Jewish rabbi, was more and more described as a celestial Being who could best be encountered not in the midst of a flesh-and-blood world but in a celestial realm. (Docetism lurked in every nook and cranny.)

Two ways of living a Christian life emerged. There was the A+ way, which meant taking vows of poverty, chastity and obedience and turning away from the evil world to live in seclusion in monasteries, nunneries and hermitages; and there was the B− way, which meant remaining in the evil world as a butcher, baker or candlestick maker, counting on the prayers of the A+ Christians to get the B− Christians into heaven.

By the Middle Ages there were two ways of attaining virtue, "The spiritual works of mercy" and "The bodily works of mercy", as follows:

The spiritual works of mercy	**The bodily works of mercy**
Converting the sinner	Feeding the hungry
Instructing the ignorant	Giving drink to the thirsty
Counselling the doubtful	Clothing the naked
Comforting the sorrowful	Harbouring the stranger
Bearing wrongs patiently	Visiting the sick
Forgiving injuries	Ministering to prisoners
Praying for the living and the dead	Burying the dead

All these works were admirable, but they were very different kinds of works.

An even more telling example of the Great Fallacy is a devotional classic from the late medieval period, Thomas à

Kempis's *The Imitation of Christ*, the full title of which is *The Imitation of Christ and Contempt for All the Vanities of the World.* The world was not seen as an arena for human fulfilment and Christian living, but as an arena so fraught with temptation that Christians should shun it and choose the divine realm over the earthly. "He who loves God," Thomas advises, "despises all other love," a conclusion that leads him to assert that love for neighbour, love for one in need, and love for a spouse are all to be spurned so that love may centre exclusively on God. "Worldly" things such as food, clothing and shelter must be used "without desire", and a similar distancing from persons is urged; God looks with favour on those who "for the love of virtue withdraw themselves from their acquaintances and from their worldly friends". It is a sign of religious devotion "seldom to see others".

The Great Fallacy made its way into the liturgy. A phrase in the baptismal service, still used by some denominations, asks the sponsors, in the name of the child, to "renounce the world, the flesh and the devil", the world and the flesh being understood as the arena in which the devil holds sway.

While the Reformation was on one level a protest against this two-tier view of reality, the above baptismal formula reminds us that Protestants soon introduced their own versions of the Great Fallacy. The traditional Lutheran doctrine of "the Two Realms", postulating an earthly realm (presided over by the state) and a spiritual realm (presided over by the church) was a reinforcement of its medieval forebears. Protestant hymnody became a fertile seedbed for dualism. Phrases such as "Let sense be dumb, let flesh retire" and references to "A joy to sensual minds unknown" have their parallels in gospel hymns:

> Earthly pleasures vainly call me,
> I would be like Jesus;
> Nothing worldly shall enthrall me,
> I would be like Jesus.

Music itself was a mixed blessing, because of its association with the sensual, the earthy, the seductive, and some Protestant groups went as far as to remove organs from their churches, fearing that the beauty of their tones would distract worshippers from the beauty of the divine Being. In Calvinist Geneva the organ pipes were once melted down to provide ammunition for the defence of the city – a curious inversion of the biblical commandment to turn swords into ploughshares. Others, not going quite that far, allowed only unison singing, fearing that the aesthetic pleasure of harmonizing would cause worshippers to stand in awe before the wonder of the human voice rather than the thunder of God's Word.

It took the wisdom of the Lutheran Johann Sebastian Bach to cut through such dead ends and fashion his most deeply moving chorale, *O sacred head, now wounded*, out of the melody of a drinking song he had heard in a local tavern. But Bach was both a genius and an exception.

Why the Great Fallacy is so appealing: a conspiratorial view

Why does the Great Fallacy persist? Some would argue that the thesis of this book is exactly backwards, and that the Great Fallacy persists because it is actually the Great Truth; life really *is* dualistic, and no attempt to argue otherwise can finally win the day. "Truth crushed to earth", as we learned in grammar school, "will rise again."

Another reason for the persistence of the Great Fallacy is that it has become so embedded in the tradition (as we have already seen) that it never occurs to people to challenge it. Traditions die hard; anything that has lasted so long must be right.

But there is another, less benign, explanation of the ongoing appeal of the Great Fallacy. Much of the support for it comes because it is in the interest of those with power – whether political, economic, ecclesiastical or all three –

to retain that power, free from challenge. To such persons a religion that centres attention on "the realm of the spirit", removed from the nitty-gritty of life, is a boon, while a religion that insists on dealing with the world of hunger, exploitation, and dehumanization is a bane. To believe, in the words of Juan Luis Segundo, that "the world should not be the way it is" is to issue a call for change, and those who benefit from "the world as it is" are going to feel threatened whenever they hear declarations of discontent.

Third world dictators want "the masses" insulated from notions of political or economic liberation, since such notions might challenge their power. They reward those within the church who preach a message to the poor that goes: accept your lot, find "spiritual" liberation in the midst of physical hardship, don't rock the boat, and God will reward you in the afterlife. When Chilean bishops challenge General Pinochet for violations of human rights, he responds that they should be in church praying.

It is not only third world dictators who feel this way. Many conservative first world Christians likewise want religion to concentrate on "spiritual" things and stay away from challenges to political or economic injustice. To opt for "spirituality" means to them that things as they are need not be challenged, whereas to suggest that the love commandment means re-examining social structures that allow people to starve is, among other things, "unwarranted interference", a distortion of the gospel, a reduction to mere politics, a replacement of Jesus Christ by Karl Marx, a humanistic rather than a theocentric faith. Many businessmen, for example, are upset by the Catholic bishops' letter on the economy because it suggests the need for changes in the capitalistic system of free enterprise.

In sum, the appeal of the Great Fallacy is that it frees us from having to face challenges to the present state of affairs. It is a way of opting for the status quo.

Now "opting for the status quo" might not be a bad thing

if the status quo were only a little more just. Those who opt for it are going to be those who most directly benefit from it. But if we look realistically at the world, we find that the beneficiaries are few in number compared to the victims, who have every reason to seek change and even more reason to be suspicious of those who refuse to do so. Those who feel the urgency of change, who believe that "the world should not be the way it is", can never rest content with the Great Fallacy; they look for ways to overcome it.

Warning: overcoming the Great Fallacy may be hazardous to your faith

But let us not proceed too fast. Overcoming the Great Fallacy, and rejoining things falsely severed, provides no automatic victories. In some cases the cure may be worse than the disease. This is particularly true in the relations of religion and politics.

The early Jews were under no temptation to equate their religion with the dominant politics of the time, since they were always the persecuted minority under attack, kicked this way and that, enslaved, imprisoned, bought and sold. They could not have equated their Jewish faith with Pharaoh's politics even if they had wanted to. However when they finally did establish a divinely approved monarchy of their own, generations later, things went to seed so rapidly that the dream of a society in which there was an equivalency between God's will and the king's decrees was a short-lived and ill-fated nightmare.

The early Christians, all originally Jews, were likewise a tiny minority at first, and it took four centuries before religion and politics became so intermingled as to be almost indistinguishable from one another. The Emperor Constantine, discovering that he couldn't lick the Christians, decided to join them and with a single stroke of the stylus made Christianity the "official religion" of the Roman Empire. State policies now began to receive religious sanction, and wars of conquest were now fought under the sign of the cross. The taste for power was so heady that for a time even the papacy had an army and fought its own wars, likewise under the sign of the cross.

When Constantine's "Christendom" began to unravel, at the time of the Reformation, there emerged the extraordinary spectacle of Europe being divided into areas whose religious affiliations were determined by the religious affiliation of their king, on the principle of *Cuius regio eius religio* (meaning roughly that if a king is Lutheran his subjects are Lutheran, ditto a Calvinist, Catholic, or Anglican).

Calvin's rule in Geneva (which often gets a worse press than it deserves and included many social programmes for the care of the sick and poor) was enforced by those fully persuaded that they knew the minutiae of God's will and could apply them to the minutiae of civil government. Michael Servetus, fleeing persecution in Catholic Europe because of his heretical views (he held that Jesus was *a* son of God but not *the* Son of God), was burnt at the stake in Protestant Geneva, just as he would have been burnt at the stake in Catholic Florence, in order that God's will be done.

Fanaticism, in other words, is not something from which religious people are automatically immune. Indeed they are particularly susceptible. One can believe that religion and politics *do* mix without being persuaded that every "mix" is a good one.

This helps us understand the new situation in the United States. During the 1960s, when "liberal" Christians were involved first in civil rights demonstrations and later in protest over United States involvement in Vietnam, many "conservative" Christians challenged the appropriateness of such activities by invoking the familiar rubric, "Religion and politics don't mix". And yet, within a decade, many of the same conservative groups where lobbying voters, and vigorously pushing political agendas of their own, such as prayer in the public schools, anti-abortion legislation, and the need for a bigger defence budget. The earlier cry "Religion and politics don't mix" was replaced by the claim that "Religion and *your* politics don't mix, but mine do".

The real issue goes: since religion and politics *do* mix, what is the nature of the mix? What sort of religion, what sort of politics? A religion that claims, according to one Southern Baptist leader, that "God does not hear the prayers of the Jews" will have important political consequences, since if Judaism is a spurious religion, its adherents can appropriately be excluded from public office in the building of a "Christian America", an agenda dear to the hearts of many religious conservatives.

With this caution in mind, we can examine some attempts to overcome the Great Fallacy.

2

Attempts to Overcome the Great Fallacy: Plan A and Plan B

What we must reconquer and reform is our entire world. In other words, personal conversion and structural reform cannot be separated.

Fr Pedro Arrupe, SJ, 1975,
while head of the Jesuit order

We have a problem. We have discovered that we apparently live in two very different kinds of worlds, worlds that can be contrasted in at least thirty-five different ways. This renders us uncomfortable. We want lives that are unified rather than fractured.

In this situation we can do one of two things: (1) By neglect or caricature or outright annihilation, we can deny the legitimacy of one of the two partners in the discussion, thus procuring victory for the other. This tactic we will call Plan A, the reduction seduction, or the "nothing but . . ." approach. Or (2) we can acknowledge that there is sufficient truth in each position so that neither one can be disposed of as easily as proponents of Plan A propose, and that the wisest course will be to bring the two positions together, in order to combine their best features. This tactic we will call Plan B, the way of synthesis, or the "if you can't lick 'em, join 'em" approach.

Let us examine each plan in turn.

Plan A: the reduction seduction, a "nothing but . . ." approach

Concern for "spirituality" renders many people nervous, particularly when it is understood as something that "really religious" people have in abundance, so that those lacking it are felt to be religiously inferior. The natural reaction in the face of such a put-down is to want to devalue spirituality, to reduce it to "nothing but . . ." an unappealing caricature that need not be taken seriously. (This is a handy device in politics as well: for example, "Capitalism is nothing but organized greed" or "Teddy Roosevelt was nothing but a jingoist.") The tactic may not be worthy, but it is widespread enough to require brief exploration. A particularly convenient put-down is to lump together everything in the practice of religion that seems distasteful, along with a few things that are exemplary, and define the result as "spirituality". William Stringfellow offers a marvellous example of this technique:

> "Spirituality" may indicate stoic attitudes, occult phenomena, the practice of so-called mind control, yoga discipline, escapist fantasies, interior journeys, an appreciation of Eastern religions, multifarious pietistic exercises, superstitious imaginations, intensive journals, dynamic muscle tension, assorted dietary regimens, meditation, jogging cults, monastic rigors, mortification of the flesh, wilderness sojourns, political resistance, contemplation, abstinence, hospitality, a vocation of poverty, nonviolence, silence, the efforts of prayer, obedience, generosity, exhibiting stigmata, entering solitude, or, I suppose, among these and many other things, squatting on top of a pillar. (Stringfellow, *The Politics of Spirituality*, p. 19)

As an accurate description of spirituality, this gallimaufry (look it up) surely misses the mark, as Stringfellow intended. But as an accurate description of the way many people view spirituality, this combination of a little truth and a lot of error is discouragingly on target.

Employing the "nothing but . . ." technique a little more systematically, we discover that those who want to discredit spirituality usually offer one or another or all of four overlapping charges:

1 *Spirituality is otherworldly.* It finds meaning in some world other than the world in which we dwell. It thereby encourages dualism (the Great Fallacy itself) by downgrading the importance of earth for the sake of heaven or exalting the sacred as superior to the secular. Thus it is escapist, for it promises salvation by extrication from the messy human condition rather than energizing us to clean up the mess.
2 *Spirituality is individualistic.* It represents the "privatization of religion" and ignores the communal dimension that relates human beings to one another. The focus is on God – a remote God somewhere else – who is to be sought singlemindedly without regard for the neighbour. It is *my* needs, the state of *my* soul, how *I* can get right with God that has priority.
3 *Spirituality is an endeavour often reserved for the élite.* It is the saints, the "holy" people, those who are withdrawn from the world, who can have the luxury of cultivating "spiritual" lives – monks, contemplatives, hermits, or people with sufficient material resources not to have to worry about where their next meal is coming from.
4 *Spirituality produces no impetus to work for change.* Since the world is evil to begin with, and salvation is found by escaping its clutches and getting attuned somewhere else, the important thing is to concentrate on that "somewhere else" and forget the world. As a result, people who are "into spirituality" aren't usually socially concerned. At best they support the status quo by default and take little or no responsibility for those who are being hurt by it, such as the two thirds of the human family who go to bed hungry every night.

If the above seems like a caricature, which it is, we need to remember that a caricature always contains enough truth to be worth attention. In order to be fair, however, we must expose "liberation" concerns to the same kind of scrutiny. In this area as well, the "nothing but . . ." approach has been employed in devastating fashion. Indeed we can construct an almost mirror image of the appraisal of spirituality.

Concern for "liberation" renders many people nervous, particularly when it is understood as something that people who are really "with it" have in abundance, so that those lacking it are felt to be morally inferior. The natural reaction in the face of such a put-down is to want to debase concern for liberation, to reduce it to "nothing but . . .", an unappealing caricature that need not be taken seriously. (This is a handy device in politics as well: for example, "Socialism is nothing but a denial of individual human rights" or "Franklin Roosevelt was nothing but a Communist.") The tactic may not be worthy but it is widespread enough to require brief exploration. A particularly convenient put-down is to lump everything in the practice of social concern that seems distasteful, along with a few things that are exemplary, and define the result as "liberation". Since William Stringfellow does not provide a second example of this technique, we will have to create our own:

> "Liberation" may indicate capitulation to atheism, a biblical perspective, gun-toting guerrilla priests, a "preferential option for the poor", horizontalist heresy, militant activism, reductionism, commitment to the revolutionary process, belief in praxis, dependence on social analysis, leaving the church or changing the church or using the church or destroying the church or redeeming the church or all of the above, prophetic realism, Marxism with a socialist veneer, socialism with a Christian veneer, naive utopianism, materialistic obsession, solidarity with the masses, class struggle, political engagement, belief in violence, creation of "base communities", mendacity, integrity, a willingness to die for justice, and a belief that God takes sides.

As an accurate description of liberation, this gallimaufry (did you look it up?) surely misses the mark. But as an accurate description of the way many people view liberation, this combination of a little truth and a lot of error is discouragingly on target.

Employing the "nothing but . . ." technique a little more systematically, we discover that those who want to discredit liberation usually concentrate on one or another or all of four overlapping charges:

1 *Liberation is this-worldly*. It reduces religion to ethics, and debatable ethics at that, glorifying violence and class struggle. It forgets the "vertical" dimension of relationship to God and concentrates exclusively on the "horizontal" dimension of relationship to people. It thereby encourages dualism (the Great Fallacy itself) by downgrading the importance of heaven for the sake of earth, or exalting the secular as superior to the spiritual. It uses concern for the here and now as a way to escape from God.
2 *Liberation is so communally oriented* it loses sight of the importance of the individual. It is willing to sacrifice persons for the sake of a future new social order. It replaces the Gospel of Mark with the gospel of Marx. The focus is so exclusively on the need for "systemic change" that individual personal conversion is downplayed and in the struggle for the "good society" God is ignored.
3 *Liberation becomes so much an endeavour by "the people"* that the contributions of those who are not part of "the masses" are not taken seriously. A reverse élitism operates. To be poor seems to be the prime qualification for social insight, and the rich (or even the moderately well off) are scoffed at. To know where one's next meal is coming from disqualifies one from being anything but an "oppressor".
4 *Liberation puts so much emphasis on impetus for*

change that it leaves no place for the inner life. In a naive belief that the world can be radically transformed, proponents of liberation concentrate so much on external structures that they forget only changed people can create a changed society. Too much stress on the needs of the body leads to neglect of the needs of the soul. Until spiritual poverty can be overcome, the stress on human self-sufficiency will only lead to burn-out and disillusionment.

Plan B: the way of synthesis; or, "If you can't lick 'em, join 'em"

It is unlikely that proponents on either side of the Plan A skirmish are going to emerge victorious. But the very form of setting out the argument offers another possibility, with more hope of leading to a creative resolution. Since each position possesses (with whatever attendant errors) a portion of the truth, and the two portions appear to provide a fuller whole than either one can provide by itself, surely the wise thing would be to draw truths from each into a comprehensive synthesis that will give us the best of both worlds. Plan B, therefore, might have two parts and look like this:

1 *Spirituality is basic to the religious life, but it can be enriched by the contribution of liberation.*

The only place we can really begin is with ourselves, with what is going on inside of us. If we haven't got our own act together we are never going to be able to reach out and help others. It will simply be the blind leading the blind. We need to develop resources that will put us in touch with all that God can be for us, which means prayer and meditation and a disciplined devotional life. If we will take sufficient time to be open to the leadings of the Spirit – through the Bible, through the lives and examples of the saints, through times in retreat, through consultation with a spiritual director – God may be able to break down some of the walls we build to keep God out.

This is a long and arduous journey and one that will never be completed in our lifetime, but it is absolutely essential to be on that journey, if we are to know who we truly are in God's eyes, and therefore in our own. Only in this way can we become instruments that God can use for the fulfilment of the divine purposes.

As long as we are seriously trying to keep our spiritual lives in order, then *of course* we must turn outwards towards others, especially towards those in need, to share what we have found. We are not to share only one-on-one, or limit our concern to the spiritual lives of others. We need to explore the social implications of our faith, to deal with the physical as well as the spiritual needs of our neighbours, to find ways to join with them in their liberation struggles. We need to listen to them, as well as hope that they will listen to us, so that we can put our two different understandings of faith together in a whole that is more complete than either part can be alone.

But we must insist on the priority of the spiritual as the basis and resource out of which our social concerns can grow, and not succumb to premature and grandiose attempts to "change society" overnight. It is not the basic job of church or synagogue to change society. The basic job of church or synagogue is to create the individuals who can do so. A changed society will come as a result of the sustained efforts of changed individuals, and changed individuals will come to the extent that we cultivate the life of the spirit as our true contribution to human liberation. We must not succumb to the temptation T. S. Eliot describes in *The Rock*, of "dreaming of systems so perfect that no one will need to be good". We must keep insisting on the need to establish spiritual depth as a basis for all social change.

2 *Liberation is basic to the religious life, but it can be enriched by the contribution of spirituality.*

We live in the midst of a world that is really hurting. Unless we are wilfully blind, we know that there are myriad problems confronting the human family, and unless they are solved pretty soon there will be no human family at all. We face a world of hunger, unemployment, child abuse, political tyranny, economic exploitation, torture, sexual harassment, and the spectre of a nuclear war our political leaders seem willing to risk if our "national honour" is assaulted.

These and other threats are not going to go away unless we decide to attack them. Our task, therefore, is to become informed, find others who share our informed concerns, mobilize and organize. Otherwise it will be the bland leading the bland.

It is morally indulgent to postpone our engagement in the liberation struggle until we feel good enough about ourselves to stop turning inwards. We belong in the midst of the struggle. People who are dying have to be helped to stay alive; people who are hungry have to be empowered to find food and work. If we stand idly by in the midst of such situations we become complicit in their ongoing misery.

As we are involved, *of course* we need to be open to, and actively seek, the kind of resources that the spiritual quest can furnish us. We need to discover ways in which a closer relationship to God can put us into a closer relationship with our neighbours. Indeed, if we fail to do this, the immensity of the social tasks will overwhelm us and we will become dispirited, discouraged, and potential or actual victims of burnout. So while we must not diminish our social passion, we need to deepen and enrich it by the contributions of spirituality.

But we must insist on the basic responsibility of all religiously minded people to be at work on the social scene, and not let the spiritual quest deflect us from that task. People can have all the spirituality in the world, but if they don't have food and clothing and shelter and medical care, not all the spirituality in the world can compensate.

Shortcomings of the synthesis

Shortcomings? Haven't we just bridged the gap between the two polarities? Hasn't the Great Fallacy been laid to rest? What is the matter with where we've got?

"Where we've got" is certainly better than where we were. We do not have so divided a world, and the two viewpoints have more in common than we imagined. I must confess that when I began thinking about the problem of spirituality and liberation, "where we've got" thus far in Chapter 2 is where I anticipated we would be at the end of the book: spirituality and liberation are two different realities, but we have managed to relate them significantly to one another. Mission accomplished.

Unhappily for such anticipations, the mission has self-destructed and a further verdict is called for: *The Great Fallacy has not been overcome, it has been reinforced.* If Baudelaire was right that the devil's cleverest wile is to persuade us that he does not exist, the Great Fallacy's cleverest wile is to be present though undetected. For what we have done, however well-meaning our attempt, has been to accept the premise of the Great Fallacy – that there are two separate worlds to be brought together – work within the assumptions of that premise, and frame a conclusion confirming the Great Fallacy rather than displacing it. We remain walking examples of religious schizophrenia, engaged in an unending series of attempts to maintain a precarious balance between two warring elements.

This will not do. We cannot settle for a solution that merely restates the problem.

3

A Clarification: “withdrawal and return”

[Jesus] withdrew to the wilderness and prayed.
Luke 5:16

“Und now ve vill haf some yotz.”
Albert Schweitzer
to J. Seelye Bixler

[Persons] cannot be fully active except they be partly contemplative, nor fully contemplative (at least on earth) without being partly active.
The Cloud of Unknowing, a fourteenth-century tract on spirituality

Let us try another tack. There is a long tradition, by no means confined to Christianity, that stresses the importance of “withdrawal and return”. The tradition reminds us that it is sometimes important, and even necessary, to engage in “withdrawal” from the clutter and ambiguity of our day-to-day existence so that, by getting in touch with deeper realities that elude us in the everyday world, we can gain not only a new realization of who we are but a deeper realization of who God is – gifts we can then take back with us in our “return” to the immediate demands of life.

On the face of it, such a proposal seems to reinstate the Great Fallacy in spades, suggesting that there *are* two diverse realms between which we oscillate, and furthermore that the "other" realm is the really important one.

But let us not reach too premature a judgment. It may be that without reinforcing the Great Fallacy we can discover insights in the movement of "withdrawal and return" that help us relate spirituality and liberation more creatively.

Our experience

Albert Schweitzer, playing Bach on a piano in the Lambarene forest for an American visitor, J. Seelye Bixler, realizes that even unrelieved Bach can become too much of a good thing and proposes, as a brief respite, an interlude of contemporary jazz ("yotz"), before returning to "The well-tempered clavichord". Professor Bixler reports that the change of pace worked wonders in his appreciation of the concluding portion of the informal concert.

Living on a less elevated level than Bach partitas and fugues, the rest of us frequently need the refreshment of a fishing trip, or a World Series game, or a day off, or a holiday, or a movie with absolutely no redeeming social significance, simply to provide a time of relaxation before returning to the sterner stuff of daily life.

This is true of the overall rhythms of our lives as well, including the life of worship. There was great wisdom behind the provision in the Ten Commandments for a day of rest, the Sabbath, on which no work was to be done. Each week had six days for labour (a provision much of the world has since reduced to five), and the seventh day was designed to be devoted to the worship of God (a provision much of the world has since revised, transforming the "holy day" into a "holiday"). But in whatever use is made of the Sabbath or "the long weekend", we see further examples of the principle of "withdrawal and return".

The biblical experience

The biblical accounts of withdrawal are many; the experiences of Moses and Jesus provide sufficient material with which to work.

Moses, who has "withdrawn" into the desert by himself (not exactly by choice, since he is being sought in connection with a murder charge), is accorded the privilege of a theophany, or manifestation of God – a burning bush that is not consumed and from within which the voice of God is heard (Exod. 3). He is told to take off his shoes, for the place on which he stands is "holy ground". Later on the same Moses, no longer solitary but leader of a vast throng, is called by God to a solitary mountain-top experience on Sinai, where he gets some orders straight from the Deity's mouth.

The same pattern is present in Jesus' life. He frequently goes apart to pray: in the wilderness (Luke 5:16), on a mountain-top (Luke 9:28), in a garden (Luke 22:41), by himself (Luke 9:18), in the company of others (Luke 9:28). The most significant clarification of his mission occurs in the desert (Matt. 3:1–11), and the moment when his disciples discover who he really is comes when they have withdrawn to the far north to figure out their next step (Matt. 16:13–20).

In all these biblical examples the "withdrawal" is temporary; it is valuable in itself yet is also for the sake of "return". In Moses' case the mystical experience of the burning bush is not an end in itself, for the voice in the midst of the bush orders him back to Egypt to persuade an unrelenting dictator to free the slaves. As for his mountain-top experience on Sinai, the purpose of the "withdrawal" is to enable Moses to "return" as the bearer of the Ten Commandments.

In the case of Jesus, each instance of "withdrawal" is the vehicle for a "return" to new levels of activity – healing lepers and epileptics, getting into trouble by claiming to forgive sins, creating a "movement" that is bound to get him in even greater trouble, clarifying his messianic vocation in disturbingly new directions, and confronting the secular authorities in Jerusalem in ways that lead to his being trussed up – on the first-century equivalent of an electric chair.

These instances are reminders of an important truth: the "withdrawal" does not seem to be an end in itself but is for the purpose of "return". Moses does not stay on Mount Sinai thinking, now that I've found God, I'll stay up here and build a self-contained flat. He goes down the mountain to a scene that must have made him wonder whether he didn't reject the idea prematurely, for things have deteriorated badly in his absence and worshipping a golden calf has become the top priority.

Nor does Jesus remain in the wilderness, or on the mountain-top, or in the garden. When he climbs Mount Tabor with a few disciples and they are accorded a mystical vision, Peter wants to stay there and, going Moses one better, suggests the construction of *three* houses in which they can settle, rather than go back again to a scary world. Jesus will have none of it, and they return to a series of unpleasant encounters that range from dealing with an epileptic boy (see Luke 9:28–43) to getting impaled on a cross.

Arnold Toynbee, who deals extensively with withdrawal and return in *A Study of History*, is right to underscore this point: "A transfiguration in solitude can have no purpose and perhaps even no meaning, except as a prelude to the return of the transfigured personality into the social milieu out of which he [or she] had originally come" (p. 217, Somerville edn).

A single world seen two ways

But Toynbee is not fully right, and our discussion thus far might suggest that true meaning, or God, is to be sought pre-eminently in that other realm of "withdrawal" and brought back into the immediate realm of "return". If so, it would appear that the Great Fallacy has triumphed once more. So two further clarifications are in order:

1 We must recognize that what happens in the experience of "withdrawal" *can* have meaning in and of itself. That is to say, it is not to be valued only in terms of its utility for a subsequently invigorated life. It will no doubt have utility; if we experience God's love despite our unworthiness, that should lead us into a new love for persons, despite their presumed "unworthiness" in our eyes. But whether or not we respond to the divine love in that fashion does not negate the ongoing reality of the divine love, however much it may highlight the limitations of our human love.
2 The best way to understand "withdrawal and return", therefore, is to see it not as an oscillation between two different worlds, but as a way of *concentrating for a time on a part of the single world we inhabit.* That single world is too spacious in its totality for us ever to embrace it fully, even in our highest moments of ecstasy or our most earthy moments of immediate awareness. And so we try, from time to time, to bring certain parts of it into clearer focus, persuaded that the clarity achieved at one point will enable us to understand the whole more adequately. The traffic can go in many directions; a single act of human forgiveness may tell us something, hitherto hidden from our eyes, about compassion on a cosmic scale, while an act of adoration of God may unexpectedly stab us with the utter worthwhileness of a personal relationship we had been neglecting.

The point of "withdrawal and return" then, is not to "find God" somewhere else and bring God back into the here and now so that it may be invested with a meaning it did not previously have, but rather to engage in the exciting discovery that the God we thought was only "out there" is *already* "in here", and it was only our previous dimness of vision (or our sin) that kept us from such awareness. "Withdrawal and return" provides us with a fresh perspective on our world, seeing it from a different angle of vision, so that what is already here can be discerned more clearly than before. And since our vision is always faulty, the rhythm of "withdrawal and return" is an ongoing component of our lives.

A musical coda

My own experience of withdrawal and return comes not so much from retreats or long sessions of private prayer as from playing the cello, a form of spiritual exercise I regrettably did not begin to cultivate until my sixtieth birthday. There are occasions, however rare, when a phrase, or even a single note, is played well enough (perhaps even as the composer intended it) for me to experience a sense of spiritual fulfilment.

As I reflect on this specific experience in my own life, I find a number of analogies to the overall theme of withdrawal and return:

1 I frequently need reminding that the "spiritual" experience is not as withdrawn from everyday experience as I might think. A moment of musical beauty is impossible without the help of such mundane objects as a bow (made from the hairs of the tail of a horse) and strings (made from the entrails of deceased cats) over which I must draw the bow. Only in partnership with these earthy and aesthetically unappealing objects (horsehair and catgut) can beauty be created.

   Score one for the unity of God's creation, not two worlds but one.

2 In the midst of a frenetic life, there is undeniable refreshment and renewal from putting the hectic pace on hold and becoming involved in something utterly different. Furthermore I not only revel in those moments while they are happening, I have the further

pleasure of anticipating them ahead of time and recalling them when they are over. They do not exist simply in themselves but in relation to what went before and what comes after. When I leave or re-enter the pressure cooker of modern existence, it is with new resources that those moments apart have provided. While I do not desire to play the cello all the time (or at least not *quite* all the time), I am convinced that I can subsequently push a pen or operate a typewriter or relate to my grandchildren more creatively in the light of those musical moments than I would be able to otherwise.

Score another for the interweaving of the various aspects of God's creation.

3 I suggested that the moments of making music do not exist simply in themselves but in relation to what went before and what comes after. That is the truth, but once again it is not quite the whole truth. For, however infrequently they may occur, there are moments that *do* have meaning simply "in themselves", a meaning that is not dependent solely on serving the utilitarian function of gearing me up to speak more effectively at the next anti-*contra* rally. They have meaning not only because of what they are used for but also, quite simply, because of what they *are*. It is good that we can occasionally create beauty as an end in itself, and we should rejoice when that opportunity is given us. It is an added grace when such moments, complete in themselves, can also nourish us for times when beauty will be far away unless we are its carriers.

Score yet another for the unexpected gifts that come to us in the midst of God's creation.

4 Although this particular musical withdrawal, like most withdrawals, begins in solitude (for demonstrably good reasons, I try to practise only when no one is at home), it does not end in solitude. Playing alone, I soon discovered, was not enough; music is a communal experience and must be shared. So the next step was to find friends with whom to play, and I was lucky to find

a pianist and a violinist who were close enough friends to tolerate my flagrantly amateur status. After some months of playing trios together, we made the communal discovery that it was not enough just to play for ourselves. We needed to play for others, not only to share what we had come to love but also because we needed the symbiosis, the interdependence and give-and-take that is part of what it means to be human: if we gave a little to them in playing, they gave much to us in listening and carried us along by the sheer fact of their presence.

Members of the Guarnari String Quartet (to leap into a totally different musical universe) have testified that they do not like to make recordings, because for acoustical purposes they must play in an empty studio where there is no audience response, no symbiosis, to carry *them* along, such as they receive in a live performance. There, too, individual experience (practice) leads inexorably to the need for communal experience (shared performance).

Score one finally for the fact that in God's creation, however solitary we may be at the beginning, we are drawn into community at the end.

Transition: meditation on two photographs

In the midst of the hectic American presidential campaign in 1940, a relatively unknown candidate named Wendell Willkie challenged an unbeatable incumbent named Franklin Delano Roosevelt. Whatever Willkie's strengths or weaknesses, for one breathtaking moment he offered voters a new vision of reality, encapsulated in the title of his book *One World*.

Willkie's vision, far-fetched at a time when the Second World War was being waged, was that we could no longer describe our situation by saying that we lived in a multitude of competing worlds – the world of American initiative, the world of resurgent German nationalism, the world of British colonialism, the world of emerging Russian power, the world of Asian aspirations for independence. However useful such terms were, they had become too provincial to communicate our actual situation – the fact that we were all part of *one* world, the world of shared humanity.

Almost half a century later the vision still seems too far-fetched to elicit wide acceptance, and yet, if anything has become clear between Mr Willkie's time and our own, it is an increasing realization that whether we like it or not we *are* part of a single human family, and that our survival (or destruction) depends on how deeply, how radically, we appropriate that fact and take the new kinds of actions it demands of us.

In similar fashion, we have been looking at our lives as a struggle between two apparently competing worlds – for which the terms "spirituality" and "liberation" are descriptive – and we have discovered that we must find our own counterpart for a vision of one world rather than two or (as in Mr Willkie's case) half a dozen.

So crucial is this transition to a new kind of perspective that we can receive our greatest initial help by moving to a different mode of communication, meditating on the two photographs in this chapter, one by Peter Brown and one by Mark Brown, which state visually what the rest of the volume will try to state verbally.

What we see initially in Peter's photograph of the wall is a wonderful play of light and shadow, delicate, almost unearthly. There are no recognizable "objects" to distract us, only random disembodied patterns with a minimum of structure, patterns that delight us by their ethereal quality. The photographer has ushered us into what many would call the realm of the spirit.

If that were the whole picture, we would feel unambiguously uplifted, grateful that for a moment we had transcended the petty stuff of our hectic daily lives and been marvellously nurtured – before the inevitable return to those hectic daily lives.

But that is *not* the whole picture. The photographer does not give us the luxury of such a painless aesthetic experience. Instead, alongside the visionary foreground he has included an excessively ordinary background, featuring that most banal artifact of our materialistic culture, a TV set. The only way to drive the point home more incisively would be to wire the photograph for sound, so that as we were looking at the beauty of the transfigured wall we were being forced to listen to . . . a deodorant commercial.

Faced with this disturbing juxtaposition, our initial reaction is surely: why didn't the photographer crop off that jarring and intrusive left-hand sliver, thereby excluding the TV set, with its reminder of the banal, and allow us the "pure" enjoyment of unalloyed beauty?

The response, of course, is that he could have done so and chose not to. For to have done so would have been to falsify. The fact is that we do not get our beauty unalloyed, or our ethereal experiences unsullied by "the world". To whatever degree manifestations of the spirit are a possibility in our lives, it is right in the midst of the world of TV sets and deodorant commercials that such a possibility is located. There is no "pure" realm into which we can flee. If we do not have a complete picture by blocking out the disturbing left-hand portion, no more can we have a complete picture by blocking out the beneficent right-hand portion and presuming to label either of them "reality".

That may sound like bad news. But there is another side to it. If the spirit can be experienced in the trappings of our day-to-day world, then there is no place in that world in which the reality of the spirit cannot appear. We can anticipate the possibility of such a presence wherever we are, and – since the world is full of surprises – the presence may be here one moment and somewhere else the next. Five seconds after the photograph was taken the wall may once again have been an "ordinary" wall, devoid of the play of light and shadow. Part of the trick of living, it would seem, as well as of photographing, is to be on the alert for things to happen when and where we least expect them.

There is yet another thing to learn. Most photographs are counterparts of the left-hand portion only, which is, after all, what cameras normally record. But after seeing this particular photograph, with its special reminder that the two portions comprise a single whole, we can see photographs of the world of TV sets in a new way; they can remind us of what the wall communicates to us, even without the presence of the wall itself. A good photograph showing only what (since our vocabulary limps) we call the "ordinary" world will henceforth cause us to ponder: what lies behind it all? Whence the particular colour of the particular rock? Why does the shade of blue in the sky cause us to rejoice? What is the status of the beauty when no camera is recording it? Why does recorded squalor fill us with resentment and recorded beauty have the capacity to bring tears to our eyes?

What happens in such cases is that we are led beyond

Peter Brown
Houston, Texas, 1979

the photograph – or, better, *through* the photograph – to ponder the meaning of our lives. It is "ordinary" things that introduce us to the extraordinary realities, just beyond our view. The fullness of our lives includes the presence of the intangible within the framework of the tangible, so that we never have one without the other and come to realize finally that they are not two but one.

The second print, by Mark Brown (which is also a photograph but one that has been subjected to a series of dark room and hand-drawn adaptations known as the photo-intaglio and relief printing processes), reminds us that when we see a photograph (or a statue or a painting), we do not simply receive from it, we also contribute to it. There is an interplay; the viewer must participate. Different viewers will, of course, see different things in this particular photograph, sometimes far beyond what the artist may have consciously intended.

My own reading of Mark's print, for example, is to see it as a nativity scene – a conviction that gradually emerged out of repeated viewings (and also, I imagine, because I am a theologian always looking for help wherever I can find it). I see a cast of characters assembled in some kind of overarching cave. They are very different – tall, short, nondescript – but there is a unity-in-difference because the scene has a focal point. We are not immediately sure what is happening at the focal point but, stimulated by an atmosphere of mystery in what the artist offers us, we can use our imaginations. We keep asking ourselves, "What is going on here?" for the lines are suggestive rather than definitional.

For me the focal point suggests a manger and a mother, with the rest of the folk straining to see. What I like best is a sense of ecstasy expressed by hands reaching up over heads in gestures of joy and abandon and maybe even gratitude. Something wonderful is happening, and they are caught up in its wonder.

Were we there, we might feel awed to silence, experiencing a joy too deep to utter, requiring physical gestures in

Mark Brown
In Waves of Dreams (State Two)

place of sounds. On the other hand the cave might also be ringing with our shouts and cheers, our uninhibited recognition that something of great moment and great goodness was happening, and we were just lucky enough to get in on it. "Joy to the world", we might all be singing, "the Lord is come!"

So much for speculation. What is the picture "actually"? What was going on when the shutter was snapped? I happen to know the answer to that question. What was going on when the shutter was snapped was that on a California beach on a Sunday afternoon a group of artists were holding on to the strands of a huge parachute that a co-operative gust of wind had just inflated for them.

This extraordinary disparity between the "actual" subject and the wealth of imaginative possibilities that the viewer can bring to bear on the subject is another instance of how life is all of a piece and not a lot of unrelated pieces. In theological language, this is sometimes called "the sacramental principle", which means simply that a piece of ordinary stuff can be the carrier and communicator of an extraordinary reality – "an outward and visible sign", as Augustine defined a sacrament, "of an inward, invisible grace". As we will explore later, "an inward, invisible grace" (forgiveness, empowerment, a sense of God's presence) can be communicated to us by "an outward and visible" and very ordinary sign (a piece of bread, a sip of wine, a drop of water). The same principle is operating here: the birth of God's Son is brought into view by a photograph of folks enjoying a fantastically successful beach party.

If bread can confront us with God's presence, parachutes and lenses and film baths can confront us with human (and divine) birth. By caprice, it seems, connections are made – not to pull two different worlds together but to remind us that there is only one world, a world we so frequently and falsely sever.

And who knows? Perhaps deliverance from that misunderstanding is finally not caprice but providence.

PART II

Clues for Construction

WHEREIN *the Great Fallacy is further interred by examining aspects of its denial in Jewish and Christian history that lead to the possibility of an alternative*

WHEREIN *the alternative begins to take shape through an examination of the earthiness of both the form and the content of scripture*

WHEREIN *the argument is advanced by recalling the story of God's involvement in the world of the flesh, as it is variously told in Judaism and Christianity*

WHEREIN *the understanding of liturgy as encompassing all of life is acknowledged, and the sacraments ensure that "sacred" and "secular" remain inseparable*

AND WHEREIN *the gift of sexuality is affirmed as inseparable from the gift of spirituality, and it is possible to anticipate drawing these discoveries together in Part III*

4

A Clue in the Confusion: scripture

The Hebrew word erets, *meaning earth, occurs at least five times as often in the Bible as the word* shamayim, *meaning heaven.*

Abraham Heschel, *Israel: an echo of eternity*

This is what Yahweh asks of you, only this: to act justly, to love tenderly, and to walk humbly with your God.

Micah 6:8

Brueggemann, Parks, and Groome,
To Act Justly, Love Tenderly, Walk Humbly

How does the Great Fallacy fare as a way of understanding scripture? Not well at all.

The earthiness of scripture

Some people who believe in the Great Fallacy assume that a "holy" book or a "sacred" scripture will be utterly different from all other books, exempt from the limitations of an earthly perspective, so lofty in its conceptions that it will direct our eyes away from earth towards heaven, from which it presumably descended in its present form.

The only ones who can sustain this illusion are those who do not bother to examine the book itself.

If they do bother, even for a few pages, they will suffer a

rude shock. For they will discover a very earthy hodge-podge – another gallimaufry, no less:

a little philosophy but not very much
a lot of gossip, rumour, and speculation
some lofty poetry and some turgid prose
more lofty poetry and some magnificent prose
too many genealogical lists
conflicting accounts of such important items as the creation of the world
a few saints alongside a rogues' gallery of stunning proportions
a collection of 150 sacred songs almost cheek by jowl with an erotic love poem
first-hand reports of military campaigns
visions . . . and dietary laws
exacting rules of behaviour
generous promises of forgiveness and new life
snippets from personal letters
lengthy bits of correspondence
floating axe heads
exhortations
help for the beleaguered
challenges to kings
support for commoners
murder, rape, and adultery
consolation, hope, and incredible possibilities
boring legislation
consistent concern for the oppressed
myths . . . and census reports

In short, the Bible encompasses and illustrates *all* the dimensions of life – spirituality and liberation wrapped so deftly in a single passage that there is no conceivable way of separating them. This book has been cited as an authority for everything from burning people alive who were suspected of being witches to forgiving enemies and turning the other cheek when assaulted.

This is the book that Jews and Christians acclaim as the source of their knowledge of God. It is not a "spiritual" book confronting an "earthy" readership. It is as earthy as anything its readership could dream of, and then some. Conclusion: It is by means of a very human vehicle that God confronts us. No encouragement at all for the Great Fallacy.

The God of scripture ". . . in our midst"

What is true of the structure of the Bible is true also of its message. That message is not about a remote God contemplating the divine essence in self-sufficient solitude, but about an active and vigorous God who is found in the midst of all those "earthy" things of which the Bible is so full.

The Greek gods, by contrast, could be described by the word *apatheia*, remoteness or disinterestedness, qualities we associate with our English word "apathy". The opposite of *apatheia* (arrived at in Greek by removing the initial letter) is *pathos*, which means to be active, engaged, involved. And the God of the Bible, rather than being a god of apathy, is the God of *pathos*, one who is "active, engaged, involved". Rabbi Abraham Heschel, who has written compellingly on this subject, defines the divine *pathos* as "combining absolute selflessness with supreme concern for the poor and the exploited" (*The Prophets*, p. 271).

There could be no better way to emphasize the Bible's repudiation of the Great Fallacy than such an understanding. On the one hand it indicates God's presence in the midst of human struggle on behalf of victims, thereby demolishing any notion that God dwells exclusively in a separate "sacred" realm. On the other hand it makes clear that the true index of belief in such a God will be the attempt of believers to embody that same quality of *pathos*, exhibiting in their own lives "supreme concern for the poor and exploited".

Where, then, according to scripture, is such a God found? The answer is unequivocal: right in the midst of what is happening on earth – siding with the Jews against Pharaoh; empowering a country boy, a "dresser of sycamore trees" named Amos, to get up in the busiest intersection of the city of Bethel and denounce the government for cheating the poor and exploited; placing a burden on everyone to give special help to the "widows and orphans", the most oppressed and exploited people in the ancient world; making "a preferential option for the poor" (as Roman Catholic bishops in North and South America encapsulate the biblical message); prodding Nathan to call King David to account for committing adultery; assuring Shadrach, Meshach and Abednego that they need not worship pagan gods even if a fiery furnace is waiting just offstage; using the voice and life of Jesus of Nazareth to point out that the way to serve God is to serve those in need; using the pen and life of Paul to empower people to believe that "neither death, nor life, nor angels, nor principalities, nor things present, nor things to come, nor powers, nor height, nor depth nor anything else in all creation" can separate them from God's love, and that in the face of promises like these they can throw themselves into the human struggle with a little more trust and abandon than they customarily display.

God's message is never, turn away from the sinful world and find me somewhere else. God's message is always, immerse yourselves in this sinful world that so desperately needs words and acts of healing, and you will find you are not alone, for I am already there, summoning you to help me.

The Bible is a very earthy book because God is a very earthy God.

The message of scripture, a new/old view of salvation

It can hardly be contested that the basic message of the Bible is salvation. What *can* be contested is what it means to say that the basic message of the Bible is salvation.

At least two important emphases in the biblical understanding of salvation have slipped through the cracks in most contemporary discussion. The first is that salvation deals with the *whole person*, not with some presumed "spiritual" portion of the whole; and the second is that salvation is a *communal* rather than an individual reality.

When someone approaches us and says, "Brother [or sister], are you saved?" the odds are high that neither of the above biblical understandings is inspiring the query. The question either translates into "What is the state of your soul?" with the clear implication that the state of your body is unimportant, or into "How are things between you and God?" with the clear implication that how things are between you and your neighbour is unimportant. In either case the questioner is exemplifying the Great Fallacy and reintroducing a dualism that is foreign to the biblical perspective.

These misunderstandings of salvation are so widespread that we must dig into the basic meaning of the word, in order to recover a more adequate biblical understanding.

The Latin root of our English word "salvation" is *salus, salutis*, and its basic meaning (to our initial surprise but eventual gratification) is "health" or "wholeness", along with derivative meanings such as "beneficial", "salutary", and "wholesome". (Salus, it is worth noting, was the goddess of public safety in ancient Rome, and anyone who has ever tried to weave through traffic in modern Rome has, however unknowingly, offered fervent supplications to this pagan deity for sheer survival.) The Hebrew word *yesha'*, which we usually translate "salvation", has a similarly wide meaning, standing for such diverse things as happiness, wealth, prosperity, victory, and even peace.

It is this fundamental connection with "health" and healing that enables us to recapture the biblical understanding of salvation as dealing with the *whole person*. Paul Tillich, who has written widely on this point, sees salvation as the healing that overcomes brokenness and division within our lives: "Healing means reuniting that which is estranged, giving a center to what is split, overcoming the split between God and ourselves, ourselves and our world, as well as the splits within ourselves" (Tillich, *Systematic Theology*, vol. 1, p. 166, slightly modified; University of Chicago Press, 1951).

Here is a perfect rendering of the fact that salvation is an overcoming of the divisions, the "splits" as he calls them, that the Great Fallacy perpetuates.

The New Testament does not talk about "spiritual" salvation, as though the salvation or health of the body were unimportant. Indeed one of the distinguishing characteristics of Jesus' healing miracles is that they can be seen simultaneously as restoring physical health and manifesting the forgiveness of sins. To be concerned about human salvation in a biblical sense, therefore, means to be concerned not only about what is usually called "the state of the soul" but also with whether or not the persons involved have soles on their shoes.

The other misunderstanding of salvation is just as much in need of correction. This is the assumption that we are "saved" when we have worked out a private relationship with God. It cannot be contested that relationship with God is at the heart of the meaning of salvation, but it must be insisted that such a relationship is achieved *in community* – community as the milieu in which new health or wholeness is received, and community as the milieu in which the new life is lived out in relation to the neighbour.

The Bible does not tell us that God bestowed salvation on individuals – on Abraham or Sarah or Amos or Deborah – and then moved those individuals into a community. On the contrary the Bible tells us that God called a people, a community, into covenant relationship, and that individuals – Abraham or Sarah or Amos or Deborah – found the fullness of who they were by virtue of relationship to that community.

That is not, of course, the end of the road but only the beginning, for experiencing salvation in this way carries with it the responsibility of reaching out to others in ways that both image and nurture the newfound wholeness. When Jesus challenges the unscrupulous Zacchaeus, a functionary of the Palestinian Internal Revenue Service, to mend his ways, Zacchaeus does not say, "I now see the error of my ways so I'll go on a retreat and start developing a rich prayer life," though somewhere along the line that might be a good idea. Instead, he says, "Lord, I realize I've been ripping off the people with this little tax racket of mine, so what I'll do is give every one of them a four-hundred-percent return on what I extorted from them in the first place."

And it is only when Jesus sees this recognition by Zacchaeus that his relationship to God means a new relationship to the community, based on justice and the restoration of stolen property, that he says, "Today salvation *[sic]* has come to this house" (Luke 19:9).

Putting the spotlight on Micah 6:8

The diverse strands we have been collecting can be woven into a single pattern, thanks to the major contribution of a minor prophet called Micah. The adjective "minor" is a quantitative rather than a qualitative judgment; the biblical prophets are classified as "major" or "minor" according to the extent of their productivity, which is a long way of saying that Micah wrote a short book. By any qualitative measurement, however, Micah is definitely in the big time.

Micah is a small-town boy from a farm about twenty-five miles south-west of Jerusalem. As he grows up, things are falling apart both domestically and internationally – a state of affairs that almost always inspires someone to prophetic utterance. Not only is the powerful Assyrian Empire breathing down the neck of every country on the horizon of the ancient world, Palestine included, but back on the farm Micah has discovered that the city folks are grabbing power and defrauding the peasants as agribusiness takes over the small farms – a baleful story he recounts in some detail in the early chapters of his book. As a result, the rich are getting richer and the poor are getting poorer. Injustice rules not only in the marketplace and the law courts but in the houses of worship as well, where everyone is trying to bargain his or her way into God's favour by the cheapest possible route. Overt bribes, sharp manoeuvres, and sneaky calculations are the order of the day, with the inevitable result that human relationships are shattered in the process.

Micah is not pleased with this state of affairs, and he has good reason to believe that God is not pleased either. So Micah and God begin to collaborate. They make quite a team.

At the beginning of Chapter 6, our focal point, Micah joins the issue through the imaginative device of summoning Israel to stand trial in the court of the Almighty. Interestingly enough, the mountains and the hills are designated as judges in the assize, an ominous foreboding for those today who commit ecological rape against the environment without fear of reprisal. There will, apparently, be a similar day of judgment for them as well.

Throughout the preceding chapters of Micah's book, a relentless and devastating case has been built up against Israel, so that it is no surprise to be informed that "the Lord has a controversy with [Israel]" and will bring an accusation against the people (v. 2). What is surprising is the yearning, almost gentle voice with which God mounts the accusation. No fire and brimstone here, but rather a grieving Deity who has lavishly poured out love only to have it repudiated. There is a swift historical review – all the way from leaving Egypt to entering the land of promise, in two breathless verses – that centres on Israel's *failure of memory*. Israel has forgotten "the saving acts of the Lord" (v. 5). Remember . . . remember . . . is the theme of these verses. They stand almost as a paraphrase of George Santayana's remark that "Those who cannot remember the past are condemned to repeat it." And since it is clear that Israel has *not* remembered, certain consequences are bound to follow, if a verdict of guilty is returned by the court.

The mood changes as the accused respond (vv. 6–7). They do not try to deny the charge. Their tactic is as old as the earliest court of law: can we bribe the prosecutor? Can we buy off the one who is bringing the charges? Everyone has a price; what is God's? Maybe we can settle out of court by offering our best calves for sacrifice, thousands of sheep instead of hundreds, endless streams of olive oil rather than a few jars, the sacrifice of our firstborn sons in exchange for having the charges dropped.

It doesn't work. There must have been a resounding "No!" that shook the rafters of the court. And hard on its heels, an alternative is proposed. Its bite has been dulled to our ears by over-familiarity; everybody knows Micah 6:8. So let us approach this verse as though for the first time and bring to it our particular question. What does it say to us about spirituality and liberation?

"You are confused about what has gone wrong, and how to set it right?" the prophet asks. "Then listen. This is what Yahweh asks of you, only this: to act justly, to love tenderly, and to walk humbly with your God" (Micah 6:8, adapted).

This is not the outline for an article in *Reader's Digest* entitled "Three Easy Steps on the Way to Moral Rehabilitation." The prophet is *not* saying, "God asks three things of you. First, you are to act justly. Second, you are to love tenderly. And third, you are to walk humbly with your God."

What *is* the prophet saying? A helpful way to explore this question is to return to the musical image of theme and variations. A composer will often present a theme, usually a fairly simple melody, and then follow it up with a series of variations in which the theme, still recognizable, is presented in a sequence of different forms: in a minor key, in syncopated rhythm, in the bass clef with musical embroidery above it, and so on. When the piece has been completed, the original theme has a richness and depth we had not previously recognized.

Applied to the Micah passage, the analogy at first appears to limp badly, for while we clearly have three discernible variations, Micah seems to have forgotten to clue us in on the overall theme itself. We can turn this apparent liability into an asset, however, by noticing that any one of the three phrases can serve as the overall theme, with the other two phrases serving as variations. We do not have *three different assertions* being made, but one assertion being made in *three different ways*.

A strange but compelling logic is at work here. We cannot talk significantly about any one of the three phrases until we have talked about all three of them; and yet by the time we have talked about all three of them, it is sufficient to talk about any one of them, since we now perceive that it includes the other two. Put visually:

> To act justly = to love tenderly = to walk humbly with God.

Or another way:

> *to act justly* means to love tenderly and to walk humbly with God
> *to love tenderly* means to walk humbly with God and to act justly
> *to walk humbly with God* means to act justly and to love tenderly

Any starting point will do, so long as it is clear that the starting point will make no sense until its meaning includes the other concerns as well.

We could decide that *to act justly* is the place to start, a "liberation" concern if there ever was one. But acting justly is not possible unless we also *love tenderly*, for justice without love is cold and harsh and can unwittingly be the vehicle of fresh injustices (out of a concern for justice for everybody, one might say to an individual, "I will decide what is best for you"). Empowerment to act justly and love tenderly comes from *walking humbly with God*, the God whom we know to be precisely a God of love and justice, in whom our own commitments to love and justice must be grounded if they are to avoid becoming instruments for our own power and domination over others.

Or we might decide that *to love tenderly* is the place to start, since love is always the bottom line of a truly creative life. But we would soon discover that loving tenderly is not possible unless we also *act justly*, since love without justice is sentimental and naive: we can hardly be said to "love" victims of economic deprivation if we are not working to create economic structures in which their exploitation will no longer be possible. And even with the best will in the world, such attempts will founder unless we believe that love and justice are at the heart of things, grounded in a God whose very nature is to act justly and to love tenderly, things we are likewise empowered to do as we *walk humbly with God*.

Finally, lest it seem that the God part is only an add-on, we could decide that *to walk humbly with God* is the place to start – a concern of spirituality if there ever was one. But if we take seriously what that means, we will find that instead of removing us from the world, such a commitment will engage us where God is, in the midst of contemporary events, as we discovered earlier in this chapter. Furthermore the God with whom we seek to walk humbly is the God of justice who therefore empowers us *to act justly*, and the God of love who therefore desires us *to love tenderly*. And since love and justice are not two separate things in God's life, they cannot be two separate things in our lives either. So to walk humbly with God is the equivalent of acting justly and loving tenderly, and they, in their turn, are equivalents of each other. Full circle.

There is a lot of repetition in the above three paragraphs. That is exactly as it should be, since they are all talking about the same thing. Which is the whole point.

The Great Fallacy cannot even get a toe in the door.

The introduction to the verse provides a conclusion to the chapter: "This is what Yahweh asks of you," Micah begins, "*only this*."

First reaction: relief. Micah has pared everything down to three lines, and we have pared the three lines down to one idea. How splendid to have achieved simplicity in the midst of such apparent complexity.

We had better enjoy the relief while we can, however, for it is likely to be short-lived. The most exacting demands usually come in the smallest packages: "Don't be frightened," "Love your enemies," "Be faithful to your spouse," "Be perfect as God is perfect." Augustine got it down to six words: "Love, and do as you please," which sounds like a cinch until we reflect that if we *do* "love", many of the things we would otherwise "please" to do are now out-of-bounds.

So also with Micah. If the "only" thing we have to do is, let us say, to love tenderly, that is easy counsel only until we are tempted (perhaps five minutes from now) to love exploitatively or (perhaps before reading the next paragraph, which is coming up *very* soon) confront someone whom it is difficult for us to love at all, let alone tenderly.

So the passage is no simple short cut to sanctity. But it is a base from which we can go forth and make our stumbling efforts, and to which we can return when we have stumbled once too often and need to check our directions afresh.

5

The Clue Comes to Clarity: incarnation

By virtue of the Creation, and still more of the Incarnation, nothing here below is profane for those who know how to see.

Teilhard de Chardin

The Word became flesh and pitched his tent in our midst.

John 1:14, adapted

We found this man subverting our nation, opposing the payment of taxes to Caesar, and calling himself the Messiah, a king.

Luke 23:2 NEB, adapted

We have discovered that the Bible is an earthy book because its subject, God, is an earthy God, present "in our midst", in the here-and-nowness of our lives. That is a considerable claim, and we must spell it out in more detail.

The goodness of creation

In the Hebrew scriptures the claim that God is "in our midst" emerges out of the struggle of the Jews to make sense of their own history, with its frequent tragedies and its infrequent triumphs. Over the centuries they became persuaded that the God who was part of their ongoing life

– "in the midst" of droughts, wars, deportations and forced marches through the desert – had created the world in which that ongoing life took place. This was a speculative conclusion (nobody was on hand to observe the creation of the world), reached after centuries of living and dying. Our natural inclination is to assume that since the creation stories come first in the Bible, they must have come first in Hebraic reflection about God. But a good author, we need to remember, often writes the first chapter last.

The affirmation of God as Creator is a late development in Jewish reflection about God, but it is an affirmation that has persisted, centrally and powerfully, ever since. In our own discussion this means at least three things. It means that since creation is God's handiwork, *creation is good* rather than evil; that since creation is God's handiwork, *God loves it* rather than despising it; and that since creation is God's handiwork, *clear signs of God's activity will be found within it.*

What these claims have in common is a repudiation of the Great Fallacy. Creation is *not* evil, so we must not downgrade it; creation is *not* repudiated by God, so we must not repudiate it either; creation is *not* devoid of God's presence, so we must not turn away from the world to find God. On the contrary, God is seeking us within creation.

This message, firmly lodged in the Hebrew scriptures, has had continuing vitality in all strands of post-biblical Judaism. One such strand, the Hasidic movement of Middle European Jewry, is especially insistent that witnesses to God's ongoing presence can be found everywhere. It is only a matter of knowing where to look. Elie Wiesel writes:

> Every woodcutter may be a prophet in disguise, every shoemaker a Just Man [one of the thirty-six who, according to Jewish tradition, preserve the world from destruction], every unknown the Ba'al Shem [the founder of Hasidism] . . . A shepherd plays a tune – the Ba'al Shem relates him to King David. A stranger in rags provokes laughter – the Master refers to him as Abraham. (Wiesel, *Souls on Fire*, p. 33)

Such claims illustrate the basic message of Hasidism, Wiesel insists, that "God is not indifferent, and man is not His enemy" (*Four Hasidic Masters*, p. 15). We are to love God by loving one another. To celebrate humanity is to celebrate God. "Who loves, loves God" (*Souls on Fire*, p. 31).

Such claims are based on a belief that the world, as God's creation, is good, that God is still at work within it, and that God calls on us to affirm creation's possibilities and keep it going, since the creation process did not come to a halt after the six days of intense divine activity recorded in Genesis.

Conclusion: life here and now has fantastic possibilities.

The messianic hope

But to lots of people the whole idea seems far-fetched. The created order, they point out, is a far cry from being "good". It is a mess. Evil, rather than good, is in the saddle. How can Jews, history's most targeted victims, be so naive?

Naive the Jews are not. Nor are they blind to the dark side of history, since they experience more of it than any other people on earth. They realize early on that the anomalies, the contradictions, the defeats, are not going to be overcome by closing their eyes to evil or assuming that with just a bit more effort they can push it off the scene.

Recognizing that they are called to struggle mightily on the human scene, they also see with utmost realism that if there is going to be redemption for a world which, if once good, is now evil, that redemption will finally be God's doing rather than theirs. And so hope begins to take root in the ashes – hope in an "anointed one" whom God will send to set things right, a *māshīah* (rendered in English as "messiah").

There are centuries of conjecture about what the messiah will be like. Some insist on a warrior king who will annihilate the hosts of wickedness; others anticipate the return of King David or, at the very least, someone who springs from the Davidic line; a few believe that an idyllic pastoral shepherd type can transform the aforesaid hosts of wickedness into forces for good; and later on, the initially curious notion of a "suffering servant" messiah makes its way into the tradition.

For the moment, however, the fact *that* a deliverer will come is more important than exactly *who* or *what* the deliverer will be like. The promise is that "the anointed one", in whatever guise, will enter into the human situation to *transform* it, rather than leading his followers (after the fashion of the Pied Piper of Hamelin) away from the messiness of history. The messianic hope is a long-shot gamble that the mess can be cleaned up, and that God cares enough about the place where the mess has accumulated to send a messiah to work right there for its transformation rather than its destruction. Instead of scrapping the created order as a divine miscalculation, creation will be remade.

Bad news to believers in the Great Fallacy, who have already written off the created order and started looking elsewhere. But potentially good news to everybody else.

The incarnation

Things frequently get so bad in Jewish history that belief in the imminent coming of the messiah reaches a fever pitch. A group of Jews see an individual stride on to the scene so powerfully and appealingly that they think, the messiah has come at last! In almost every case, the hope is dashed: the presumed messiah gathers no followers, or his ideas go sour, or he is rudely defeated, or he turns out to be a charlatan.

On one occasion, however, a tiny group of Jews gathers around an itinerant rabbi – much like themselves, without significant schooling or cultural polish or connections in high places – and even though he meets a tragic end after a couple of years of public life (the political authorities execute him as a "subversive"), the manner of his life, the nature of his teaching, and a conviction that not even death can destroy him convince this handful of friends and associates that he is indeed the messiah they have been waiting for. His name is Joshua ben Josef or, as we now say, Jesus, son of Joseph, and they increasingly feel that in the life of this teacher from the boondocks of Nazareth – a life that includes tears and hunger and disappointment and betrayal – God has been incarnate.

The word "incarnate" is key. What it means is stated in the prologue to the Fourth Gospel, which contains some real surprises. It starts out non-threateningly enough with an abstract claim that "In the beginning was the Word", "Word" being an unfortunate translation of the Greek *logos*. *Logos* is a word that has had many meanings. To first-century readers living in a Greek culture – the Gospel's most likely target – it seems to have represented a mediating principle between the eternal realm of goodness and the temporal realm of evil. If so, the Gospel's readers were in for some surprises, for the author immediately claims that the *logos* was not only "with God" but "was" God. And after several verses of equating the activity of the *logos* with the activity of God, the author then takes an unexpectedly new tack and asserts unequivocally that the *logos* became flesh and pitched his tent in our midst (John 1:14), which means that the *logos* took up habitation among us, became like us, shared our plight.

Nothing could have been more shocking to the first readers of the Fourth Gospel. Believing that the world was impure and that "flesh" was the seat of its impurity, they could not have conceived of anything divine becoming "flesh". And yet that is exactly what the author of the Fourth Gospel asserts. The Latin word for "flesh" is *carnis* (from which we get words like "carnivorous", meat-eating or flesh-eating, and "carnal", which we associate with "desire", which, when preceded by "carnal", we associate with the risqué). Incarnation means "in the flesh", and to say that God was incarnate is to say that God was "in the flesh"; that is, in a human life fully like ours, no exemptions granted.

Incarnation, in other words, is not about a divine masquerade, in which God appears to live a human life but really doesn't. It is about a God who is found in the midst of life in the flesh, in a human life like ours, subject to all our limitations, frustrations and anxieties. We need not seek God elsewhere, for God has already sought us right where we are.

So we can no longer speak of God without speaking of humanity, since it is in a human life that we see God most clearly; and we can no longer speak of humanity without speaking of God, since humanity is where God's tent is pitched.

This claim that the messianic hope was fulfilled in Jesus of Nazareth divides Christians and Jews, and we must take note of the tragic history that has resulted.

The first "Christians" were a tiny group of Jews who gave Jesus the title of "Messiah" (for which the Greek equivalent is "Christos"). Most first-century Jews did not share this belief, and the Christians soon turned to the Gentile world to expand their fellowship. But as soon as they began to get a little clout on the political scene, they started making things extremely rough for Jews who did not agree with them. In the name of one who came preaching love, they practised hate, calling Jews "Christ killers", a "deicide race", "apostates", and a good many other things less esoteric and more blunt. They subjected Jews to ghetto life, torture, forced conversion and death.

This is a scandalous legacy. Not only must Christians repudiate it, but they must begin to look at the relation of Jews and Christians to the messianic claim in a new way.

Jews and Christians still share a messianic faith. That has not changed. What has changed is that (if one may so put it) they now have different timetables: Christians await the "second coming" of a messiah who for Jews has not yet appeared.

Jews have waited millennia for a messiah. Their ongoing agonizing question is, "Since the world is so evil, why does the Messiah not come?" With every reason to give up hope, they persist in affirming that, though he may tarry, yet will they wait for him.

Christians have frequently responded to Jews in the following manner: "You have a problem? Fortunately for you we have a solution to your problem. The Messiah *has* come. All you need to do is become Christians and believe the good news." This approach has led to an escalating Christian "triumphalism" that finally ends up vilifying Jews for their persistent disbelief.

Christians are not entitled to operate this way. For if Jews have a problem with messianic faith, so do Christians. The traditional Christian "answer" engenders a question of its own, the opposite of the Jewish question, that goes: "Since the Messiah has come, why is the world so evil?" Christians have assumed that the cosmos got tidied up around AD 30 and that the message ever since has been one long victory communiqué. Christians need to learn that the redemption of the world is not so evident to Jews (and many others) as it apparently is to some Christians. "We taste its lack of redemption on our tongues", states Martin Buber.

There are no cheap triumphal choruses for Christians – or for God. Auschwitz put an end to them. So, long before, did the first unjust death of a child.

Jesus of Nazareth

The claim *that* there was an incarnation is a further nail in the coffin of the Great Fallacy. But we must press on to explore briefly *who* was incarnate and *what* the incarnate life was like.

Let us suppose for a moment that we do not know the

Jesus story, and that we are asked in what kind of life we would expect an incarnation of God to take place. We would be likely to assume that it would occur in the most impressive manner possible, in someone well enough placed in public life to assure maximum exposure to the claim, and in a place where the most people with the most influence could spread the word around.

But according to the biblical story, it didn't happen that way at all. Jesus was born in a tiny town off the beaten track, in a barn rather than a hospital. His mother was under suspicion of having had an affair, and it was rumoured that his "father" was not the biological father; the "parents" came from a working-class background, and both of them were Jews, a scattered group well towards the bottom of religious census charts. Not a very prepossessing set of claims.

Consider now the cover of this book and ask, "Where are the signs of God's presence in the picture?"

Some might respond, "In the beautiful world of nature – the lake, the cloud-flecked sky, the islands, the invisible power of the wind that the sailing boat suggests."

Someone with an eye to symbolism might respond, "In the bird flying in the sky, a dove, symbol of the Holy Spirit."

Another, sensitive to a different kind of symbolism, might say, "In the carpenter's square on the post, which represents the order and stability of God's universe."

Still another, schooled in certain ways of picturing God, might respond, "In the man with the beard, who is obviously in charge of the whole operation and is issuing the orders."

Hardly anyone would be inclined to answer, "In the little boy with the long hair, sandals, blue shorts, and T-shirt." The idea seems almost offensive.

Add the further "offence" that the scene of the painting is Nicaragua – the land to which an American President has sent massive shipments of arms that kill children like the child in the picture – and we get a further sense of the way the Jesus story breaks the limits of anything we can anticipate or control. About the only thing that could make the story more unlikely would be to portray the Messiah as a woman – as does a gripping modern portrayal of the crucifixion entitled *Christa.* And if that proposal seems far-fetched to some people today, we need to reflect that it is no more far-fetched than the proposal that the Messiah was the son of a Jewish carpenter seemed then.

The Messiah did not come in the way people expected. Anybody writing the script in the first century would surely have done it differently. There would have been none of this "particularity" of a Jew, a working-class type, a man getting hungry and thirsty. There would have been a messiah who transcended all that, who was exempt from suffering and change, as befits a god, who gave gentle maxims and helped people immunize themselves against the hurts and passions of the world – a reassuring phantom from another world who could give directions for shedding this world and entering the one from which he came.

In the face of such a proposal, there is one thing of which we can be sure: The boy in the carpenter's shop is not an otherworldly phantom; when he misses the nail and hits his finger with the hammer, it hurts. And when it becomes clear to him, about thirty years down the line, that he has some kind of special mission to perform, he is simply himself so fully that God can be seen through who he is and what he does. People see a rabbi who somehow personifies the God he talks about – a God who forgives, a God who heals, a God who comforts, a God who chastises, a God who challenges, a God who gives, a God who shares the human lot. That single unified life is not a fusion of two dissimilar things but an integrated whole. All that we mean by "spirituality" at its best is present in him; all that we mean by "liberation" at its best is present in him, and they cannot be separated. This is a consistent pattern throughout his ministry. For example:

1 Early on, Jesus and his followers come to a field of grain. They are hungry. But it is the Sabbath. A dilemma: no work can be done on the Sabbath, and plucking grain counts as "work" – a splendid occasion to drive home a "spiritual" lesson about the observance of ritual law. But Jesus, who believes that human beings are "the temple of God", tells his followers to fill their stomachs, Sabbath or no. Seeking to explain this unforeseen decision, Frei Betto, a Brazilian priest, comments:

> There is nothing more sacred than [a person], the image and likeness of God. The hunger of [a person] is an offence to the Creator . . . A religion that cares for the supposed sacredness of its objects but turns its back on those who are the real temples of God the Spirit, is worthless. (Betto, *Fidel and Religion*, pp. 53–4)

2 Midway through his ministry, during a "retreat" of five thousand people, far from any supermarkets or delicatessens, it is suddenly supper time and everybody is ravenously hungry, particularly the children – a great opportunity for Jesus to say something like, "Let us ask God for strength to rise above our rumbling stomachs and show our true devotion to 'the things of the spirit' by fasting all night long." But instead of such an exhortation he enlists the help of the children and busies himself with finding ways to provide an evening meal.

3 Almost at the end of his ministry, Jesus gathers his closest followers in an upper room for the celebration of the Passover. How should they prepare for such a time of solemn worship? Prayer, meditation, fasting, interior examination are traditional exercises. Which does Jesus propose? None of the above. Instead he gets a towel and a basin of warm water and makes the rounds of the room, washing the dirty smelly feet of sandal-shod disciples who moments before had been

walking through dust and donkey dung – a demeaning task that must have seemed curiously out of keeping with the exalted service of worship that lay just ahead.

Since we don't *wash* feet in public any more, the closest analogue in our experience would be to massage the feet of our dinner guests, or do whatever else was appropriate for their physical comfort. Whatever we did, it would indicate that nothing is so important that physical realities lose their importance. "At the end of his life," as Juan Luis Segundo puts it, "Jesus found nothing of greater value than to kneel at the feet of these poor men, his friends" (cited in Alfred T. Hennelly, *Theologies in Conflict*, p. 148; Maryknoll, NY, Orbis Books, 1979).

Dealing with cracked toes becomes an act of worship.

These three randomly selected examples from Jesus' ministry all turn out to involve food. Joseph Grassi can go as far as to say of one of the Gospel writers, "Luke is almost obsessed by the centrality of food and drink in the ministry of Jesus" (*Broken Bread and Broken Bodies*, p. 55). We can go farther than that: the whole Bible shares this "obsession", from the disastrous eating of the fruit of the tree of the knowledge of good and evil, in the book of Genesis, to the final triumphant messianic banquet in the book of Revelation. The highest moment in the worship of God comes when bread and wine are passed around. And one of the ultimate tests of an authentic life, according to Jesus' moral calculus, is whether or not we gave food to the hungry person.

This unwillingness to separate the human being into two parts ("body" and "soul", or "spirit" and "flesh") is evident not only in what Jesus did but also in what he said. Both the *way* he taught and *what* he taught illustrate this, as we discover in his teaching about God's realm.

Jesus' *way* of talking about God's realm, particularly in his parables, does not involve his saying, "If you want to understand God's realm, close your eyes and turn your back on the world, since it can only confuse your vision. Put out of your mind all the images of ordinary living, and then maybe you can get an inkling of what I'm talking about."

His method is just the opposite. The images he uses to describe God's realm are always drawn from the world around him:

> God's realm? Well, imagine yourself getting all geared up to buy a piece of real estate. Remember how that feels? . . . And that widow down the block who thought somebody had stolen her Social Security cheque. Remember how happy she was when it turned up? . . . And that father in Perth Amboy whose youngest son flew the coop and blew the whole trust fund, principal *and* interest, that his father had created for him. Remember how the father used to go down to the bus terminus every day, just to see if by chance his son had returned? And how ticked off the older brother was when his younger sibling did return, flat broke, and the old man threw a party for him? . . . And remember that middle-management executive trying desperately not to get fired, by doctoring the books, currying favour with the boss in order to avoid a hostile takeover? We can learn even from that misguided zeal.

If it's clues you want about the nature of God's realm, Jesus tells us, start looking right in front of your noses, because it is out of the bits and pieces of what you find there that you'll get whatever clues there are. So take it seriously, he might go on, when you see people reunited with children they thought they had lost for ever, or when some day, somewhere, somebody – maybe even you – recovers something precious that had got lost, or you put the leftover Chablis in the bottle of Chenin Blanc and it doesn't work. The pointers don't mean that God's realm has come in all its fullness, but they do mean that it is breaking in here and there – and that when it *does* come in all its fullness, those pointers will turn out to have been the best previews in town. Never forget, he might conclude, that you saw it here first, in the kitchen or out in the garage or just around the corner.

Even more important than the *way* Jesus taught is *what* he taught. The content reinforces the claim that God's realm, like God, is "in our midst". From the moment in Mark's Gospel when Jesus bursts abruptly on to the scene, he has stunning news on his lips. First recorded utterance: "God's realm is at hand", which can also be translated: "is in your midst", "has broken in", "is right here and now". The world isn't suddenly transformed into God's realm the moment he speaks those words, but from that moment on the world has to be looked at in a new way, not as alien territory to be shunned or only warily entered but as a homeland to be embraced in joy, since it is the arena of much more than meets the eye, and all the ordinary things going on around us are full of a significance we had not previously imagined. Joan Chittister captures the new mood perfectly in the *National Catholic Reporter:* "The journey to God becomes less a process of tiptoeing through a minefield in snowshoes, and more a pilgrimage in spring."

"You want to talk about God's realm," somebody back then might tell us, "then talk about sheep, or widows, or wineskins, or patched-up coats, or people working on a construction job. The signs are all around you. Open your eyes! Open your ears! Open your hearts!"

That's not the whole message, of course. God's realm is not just an extension of our realm, presented in living Technicolor on a wide screen. For the other side of the message is that the further creation of God's realm is a vast reconstruction project, already under way, in which we are God's concern. Jesus did not come to bless our failings, but to let us in on the ground floor of what one of his later followers called "a more excellent way". The word in Mark after the announcement that "God's realm is at hand" is "Repent!" which means "Turn about, start all over again, make a clean break with the past." There is a shattering as a condition of rebuilding.

We need to notice one other troubling thing about the message Jesus brings. Who are the people to whom the good news is particularly directed? The answer can only be sobering to people who read (and write) books like this, for the message is particularly directed to the poor, the outcast, the people who have AIDS, the laid-off workers, the women, the folks on welfare. They all appear likely to make it into God's realm considerably before the rest of us. Rich young rulers are also welcome, of course, but some strings are attached to their entrance; they – read "we" – have more encumbrances to get rid of first.

Our carefully contrived social barriers, for example, skilfully erected to keep us at a good distance from those of a different race or social class or economic background, collapse like a house of cards the minute we take seriously the announcement that God's realm has broken in. And all the efforts that have gone into creating those barriers – economic systems based on greed, nuclear weapons based on fear, privileges for the few based on self-concern – likewise crumble and have to be replaced.

It's enough to make one wish the Great Fallacy were true. Then at least we wouldn't have religious leaders interfering in our lives.

6

Acting Out the Clue: liturgy and sacraments

They beheld God, and ate and drank.
Exodus 24:11

When I give people food, they call me a saint. When I ask why there is no food, they call me a communist.
Dom Helder Câmara,
Archbishop of Recife, Brazil

Only those who cry out for the Jews have the right to sing Gregorian chant.
Dietrich Bonhoeffer, during the persecution of the Jews in Germany

[The liturgy] turns our hearts from self-seeking to a spirituality that sees the signs of true discipleship in our sharing of goods and working for justice.
US Catholic bishops' pastoral letter,
para. 331

Liturgy. We feel relieved; here at last is a topic removed from activism and exhortations to change the world. For a moment we can leave the bustle, seek nourishment, and ground our lives in communion with God, before returning to the fray. Right?

Liturgy as "the people's work"

Wrong. Or, at most, only partly right. For if there is any portion of our faith that challenges the Great Fallacy (lurking behind every word in the previous paragraph), it is a true understanding of liturgy.

Our English word "liturgy" is a transliteration of the Greek word *leitourgia*, which in turn is a combination of two Greek words, *laos* (from which we get "laity" or "the people") and *ergon* (from which we get "erg", a unit of work, as we all learned in high school physics). "Liturgy" therefore is simply "the people's work" or "the work that people do". When first used, it had nothing to do with religion or theology or church or worship. It meant "the work that people do *wherever they are*".

Paul, for example, uses the closely related word *leitourgoi* (meaning "servants" or "ministers") to describe the pagan tax collectors (Rom. 13:6). They were not servants or ministers in the church, but in the government, and their service or ministry – their "work" – was not to lead the Wednesday evening prayer meetings but to run the Internal Revenue Service of the Roman Empire as efficiently as possible.

"Liturgy", then, describes what people do in a place of business, in a shopping centre (whether buying, selling, or just looking), in the defensive backfield of the San Francisco Forty-niners, in a physics laboratory, giving birth to a child, being a track coach, writing a book, hauling garbage to a dump site, serving in the state legislature, or being a yeoman third class in the US Navy.

Gradually, in what must be viewed as a succession of linguistic impoverishments, this original meaning of the word was narrowed until it came to mean what it means today in the popular mind, "the work people do *in church*" whether praying prayers, singing hymns, preaching sermons, distributing communion, receiving communion or struggling to stay awake.

This kind of narrowing breathes new life into the Great Fallacy, for it legitimizes a tidy distinction between what happens "inside church" and what happens "outside church". There is a sacred realm and a secular realm, and never the twain shall meet.

Only by recapturing the original meaning of liturgy can we avoid such a mistake and validate our contention that life is all of a piece and that "worship" and "action" are finally only different ways of talking about the same thing.

Worship and worth-ship

Before proceeding full steam ahead with this discovery, however, we need to take account of a possible wrong turn. It would be misleading to leave the impression that worship is an activity designed solely to energize us either for social change or inner contentment. This is the "filling station" view of worship: we need a full tank of petrol once a week to keep us moving along life's road, and we need to have the battery checked in order to see the road clearly, particularly in the dark. The purpose of Sunday is to keep us fit Monday to Saturday.

There is some truth to this view. We do get tired and our vision does falter, and we need help wherever we can get it. But such a utilitarian view of worship reduces it to little more than a device or gimmick, which, if we were strong enough, we could probably get along without.

So we need to remember that the fundamental reason to worship God is that God is worshipful. "Worship" after all, simply means "worth-ship"; worship is an acknowledgment of the worth-ship of God. Whether it yields tangible "returns" or not, worship is a significant human activity. Part of what distinguishes human beings from other forms of life is not only that we make tools (*homo faber*), play (*homo ludens*), work for a living (*homo laborans*), make lifetime commitments with partners (*homo amans*), and use our analytical minds (*homo sapiens*), but also that we worship (*homo adorans*).

Confusion arises, however, when we see "work" and "worship" as two quite different "liturgies", rather than seeing them as two expressions of the same "liturgy"; that is, as the work we do wherever we are at the moment, part of which may be done in church and part elsewhere. Jesus' picture of the Last Judgment makes clear that feeding hungry persons is a way of worshipping God (Matt. 25:31–46). And in the Sermon on the Mount he makes the point that if we approach the altar fresh from an unresolved battle with a brother or sister (meaning anybody), we cannot make an offering to God in those circumstances; we must put the gift down, leave the altar, and be reconciled with the brother or sister (still meaning anybody) before we can return and offer the gift to God (Matt. 5:23–25). To honour one made in the image of God (by patching up the quarrel) is already to honour God; to be in right relationship with God (by offering a gift at the altar) necessitates being in right relationship with brother and sister, which means already to be in right relationship with God.

The argument sounds circular; it is a glorious circularity.

Reclaiming old forms in new ways

So isolated has much worship (in church) become that it is tempting to suggest taking a new liturgical broom, sweeping clean, and starting all over again. Jesus, however, warns us of the perils of the "empty house"; just as we are disposing of all the debris out the front door, seven devils are sneaking in at the back (Matt. 12:43–45). Newness is no guarantee of improvement.

We can never make a fully clean break with the past. Such things as who our parents were, the good and the bad in our upbringing, the culture into which we were born (without being consulted) indelibly shape us. Some events from the past need to be repudiated, some affirmed, and not a few reinterpreted. This is true of worship as well. Bad hymns can be replaced by good hymns, droning prayers by vital prayers, actions that ignore the world by actions that affirm it. Sometimes even preaching can come alive.

This recuperative power can be illustrated by observing how an act of individual "devotion", the Roman Catholic stations of the cross, can be invested with new life and show us that spirituality and liberation are two sides of the same liturgical coin.

Early Christians in Jerusalem used to re-enact Jesus' carrying the cross from Pilate's court to Golgotha. Churches elsewhere gradually began to provide facsimiles of the stages or "stations" on the journey ("Jesus falls the first time", "Jesus is nailed to the cross", and so on), by depicting them on church walls. Individuals would stop before each of the fourteen stations for appropriate prayers and a time of private nurturing.

This would hardly seem the stuff out of which the relationship of worship to social transformation could be re-established, and yet Leonardo Boff, a Brazilian Franciscan, has created a new setting of the stations that not only focuses on the "then" but relates it vividly to the "now".

His treatment of the sixth station ("Veronica wipes the face of Jesus") provides an example. Back "then" a woman named Veronica, an early follower of Jesus in Jerusalem, broke through the crowd of soldiers and gently wiped the sweaty and bloody head of Jesus in an exemplary act of human compassion. Worshippers kneeling in front of this depiction would feel gratitude that she was on the scene, perhaps meditate on the need for similar compassion in their own lives, and then move on to the seventh station ("Jesus falls the second time").

Boff lingers. While he is there, he pulls the "then" into the "now". He first reminds us of our conventional question, "Where do we find God?" and our conventional answers: in prayer, the interior life, asceticism, the church, the sacraments, loving encounters with neighbours. But there is a more important question: "Where does God want to be encountered by human beings?" Boff offers two answers. First God chooses to encounter us in Jesus Christ, a conventional enough answer until we realize that in this very station Christ is being portrayed as "a frail, powerless human being". We must be "scandalized" at the thought of God being in such a situation. But there is more to come:

> Second, we encounter God
> in the lives and faces
> of the humiliated and downtrodden.

What is the new mindset of "the humiliated and downtrodden"? It is an unwillingness any longer to accept their lot passively. These people, with whom Jesus identifies himself:

> raise a protest:
> This situation contradicts the will of God,
> and is unacceptable to any human being
> who has preserved the least trace of
> humaneness.

But in addition to raising a cry of protest, the downtrodden are also

> the bearers of a great hope
> which manifests itself as a demand of justice.

They expect "to recover their trampled dignity", and they claim God's support:

> God considered this hope and this demand of
> justice so ineradicable
> That [God] identified with the oppressed.
> In their faces we find the face of God.

What has all this to do with Veronica and our own response to what she did?

> If we want to serve the true God . . .
> then we must do as Veronica did.
> We must break out of the circle of
> self-absorption
> and pay heed to the bloodied face
> of our fellow human beings.
> For they are the great sacrament of God,
> the signs and instruments of authentic
> divine reality.
> If we do not share life with the oppressed,
> we do not share life with God . . .
> When we wipe the face of our fellow
> human beings
> who are suffering life as a painful passion,
> we are wiping the face of Jesus.
> (Boff, *Way of the Cross – Way of Justice*, pp. 42–8)

Boff is not arguing only for individual gestures of compassion after the damage has been done. To wipe the face of our fellow human beings means examining why our fellow human beings are suffering; discovering what political, social and economic structures cause their suffering; exploring what kinds of systemic changes will be needed to ensure that the suffering does not continue; reflecting on how we can avoid slipping back into the old oppressive structures once the zeal for change abates. Such concerns are mandatory for Christians, since the story of Jesus' suffering and the story of all human suffering are part of the same story.

The title of Boff's book reads *Way of the Cross – Way of Justice*. Maybe the "–" should be an "=" sign.

Sacramental subversion

"Subversion" is a scare word in our vocabulary. It calls to mind spies, cloak-and-dagger operations, covert plans to overturn a government. The word literally means "to overthrow (*vertere*) from below (*sub*)". Where we least expect it – from below – movements may be generated that bring about radical change in the ordering of society.

But surely such movements will not be generated around a communion table. What could be more remote from "liberation" than a kind of "spirituality" in which a bunch of people are eating morsels of bread and taking little sips of wine? Here is a place where the sacred and the secular appear fully insulated from each other. No "overturning" is going to be initiated here.

Those who so believe need to look again. For the time at which the Christian community proclaims (with whatever differences of interpretation) the "real presence" of Christ is not a time of ignoring the world outside but of incorporating it by making use of its creations. This "sacred" experience cannot even occur without the use of earthy objects from the here and now namely bread and wine. And the bread and wine are available only because there has been planting, cultivating, harvesting, gathering, fermenting or baking, storing, transporting, distributing, buying and selling – in short, all those things we identify with the life of economics and politics. The so-called "sacred" is not realized without the help of the so-called "profane". There is no point at which the attempt to separate them has more difficulty than right here.

The process works both ways. While we do not live "by bread alone", as Jesus informed the tempter in the wilderness, neither can we live without it. To say "We are not saved by bread *alone*" is an appropriate reminder to those with full stomachs. To say "We are not saved *without* bread" is a necessary acknowledgment of the claims of those with empty stomachs, and a rallying cry to find ways to procure the needed bread.

The Eucharist (as Tissa Balasuriya points out in *The Eucharist and Human Liberation*) was originally a celebration of the political and economic liberation of the Jews from Egypt. The early church had a vigorous view of the relationship between liturgical integrity and commitment to the poor. Hear Basil the Great (AD 330–379):

> The bread in your cupboard belongs to the hungry [person], the coat hanging unused in your closet belongs to the [person] who needs it; the shoes rotting in your closet belong to the [person] who has no shoes; the money which you put in the bank belongs to the poor. You do wrong to everyone you could help but fail to help. (Cited in John Ryan, *Alleged Socialism of the Church Fathers*, p. 9; St Louis, B. Herder, 1913)

Back then, it would have been self-evident that food on the Lord's table cried out for a world in which there was ample food on all other tables.

Later Christians, however, tamed and domesticated the event, so that rather than remaining a celebration of full liberation for all people, it was pressed into the service of the status quo and became a resource for inner calm rather than outer change. This "social conditioning of the Eucharist" has relieved the consciences of leaders of repressive regimes from any necessity to act on the radical social consequences of a meal that is supposed to pave the way for adequate food for all, rather than insulating comfort for a few. The potential for prophetic action was turned into non-threatening inaction. Colonialism and industrialization later increased the distance between the eucharistic table and other tables and rendered the Eucharist more and more irrelevant to the lives of the poor, who saw the liturgy supporting those in power and speaking no word of admonishment to them.

From such a perspective the latent explosive power at hand when the Eucharist is celebrated is beyond calculation. Dictators, who have tried to suppress preaching as politically dangerous and Bible study as potentially subversive, have often let the church go on celebrating the apparently innocuous rite of the breaking of the bread. In terms of their own self-interest they are making a great mistake, since the "simple" act of breaking bread at the Lord's table empowers people to engage in the more complex act of breaking structures of oppression that perpetuate the lack of bread elsewhere.

Paul's difficult warning that we can eat and drink at the Lord's table to our own damnation (1 Cor. 11:27–29), has been the object of centuries of speculation. The foregoing discussion suggests that one way of eating and drinking to our own damnation may be to accept food from the Lord's table without making sure that there is food on other tables.

The usual interpretation of sacrament goes like this: We go through our daily, dreary, ordinary routines, and every once in a while there is an unusual or extraordinary event – a baptism or a Eucharist with a special meaning – that for the moment intrudes the presence of the unusual, the extraordinary, into the daily routine. And after that we settle back into the routine, glad for our momentary respite.

But surely it is the other way around: the sacramental moments are meant to be the normative moments that show us what ordinary life is meant to be and usually is not. On this reading, it is all of life that is included in the "real" moments, the sacramental moments. The Lord's Supper is not meant to be the extraordinary meal but the *ordinary* one, the meal that is the model for all other meals. The way bread is shared on this occasion is the way bread is meant to be shared on all other occasions. The dynamics of the occasion say to us:

> You can't afford to pay for the meal? Come anyway, there is no charge. You don't usually meet the sort of people who are gathered here? Come anyway, for there are no distinctions here between upper and lower classes, rich and poor, male and female; everyone is on the same footing, and the equality is an equality of need. You haven't done anything to earn the right to be here? Come anyway, for neither has anybody else.

And when someone replies that it isn't really like that, since at many tables women cannot yet preside, or minorities aren't really welcome, let it be said that such a recognition, loudly noted, is itself an important step on the way to closing the gap between what is and what is meant to be.

Discovering that one moment has potential for all other moments is by no means limited to the sacraments. Other kinds of special moments, often fleeting, are pointers to what all moments could become. Couples in love give flowers to one another. The simple act expresses in that moment what is meant to be true of all the other moments, namely that life is a giving and receiving, pre-eminently the gift of each self to the other, which the flowers symbolize. The flowers will fade and die; that does not really matter. What matters is that for a moment they have expressed what will not fade and die – the love of two persons for each other, and their affirmation that all moments are meant to contain the sort of giving and receiving symbolized in that particular moment.

The play within the play: help from *Hamlet*

The sacraments, as the supreme expression of this, have a significance similar to the significance of the play within the play in *Hamlet*. In Shakespeare's drama things get all mixed up. No one is quite sure who the heroes and villains are, who should be trusted, who should be doubted, what has "really" been happening. And so Hamlet decides to present a play within a play. He will put on a dramatic production for the king that will reveal what is *really* going on. The play within the play becomes the moment of truth, as a result of which the other moments can be seen with fresh clarity.

So too with the sacraments. While *Hamlet* shows us what is evil, the sacraments show us what is good. They represent those moments of truth that tell us, confused as we are by all other evidence, what is *really* going on, what the nature of life is meant to be. And the nature of that life, we learn, has everything to do with justice and nothing to do with injustice; everything to do with possibilities for the *whole* person and nothing to do with dividing persons into bodies and souls so that liberation can be neglected for the sake of spirituality, or vice versa; everything to do with "calling into the present" one who comes, in the words of an Advent hymn, with a clear agenda of liberation:

> He comes to break oppression,
> To set the captive free,
> To take away transgression,
> And rule in equity.
>
> He comes with succour speedy
> To those who suffer wrong;
> To help the poor and needy
> And bid the weak be strong.

Full-blown subversion.

7

A Case Study: spirituality and sexuality

And I wanted to cry out at her that I could not put the body apart from the soul, and that the comfort of her body was more than a thing of the flesh, but was also a comfort of the soul, and why it was, I could not say, and why it should be, I could not say, but there was in it nothing that was ugly or evil, but only good. But how can one find such words?

Pieter van Vlaanderen, in Alan Paton,
Too Late the Phalarope

Pieter's wife is unable to believe that human sexuality can be a good thing. By seeking to distinguish between the soul (goodness) and the body (evil) she is affirming the Great Fallacy without knowing it and demonstrating its baleful consequences. In so thinking she is not alone, for there is a strain of Christian teaching (to which she has obviously been exposed in her upbringing) that conditions her to feel this way and ultimately contributes to the tragic destruction of her marriage.

A fresh look at spirituality and sexuality can help us see some further consequences of the Great Fallacy and also provide resources for overcoming it.

Spirituality and sexuality at odds: a long history

When it comes to sex, Christianity has had a bizarre history. The Hebrew scriptures, which Christians inherited, do not contain the negative view of sex that has clouded much Christian history. The Song of Songs, for example, is a collection of oriental love poems with considerable erotic imagery. Later Christian interpreters tried to disguise its real subject by suggesting that it was really an allegorical poem about Christ's love for the church – a notion that would have startled its original authors, since they wrote at least three hundred years before Christ's birth.

The basic Jewish view (which took a back seat when Christians started interpreting the Jewish scriptures) can be found in the creation story: after each specific act of creation (earth, vegetation, sun and moon, birds and sea monsters, cattle and creepy-crawlies) there is the refrain "and God saw that it was good" (see Gen. 1:10, 12,18,21,25). But after creation hs come to its culmination in the creation of male and female, after sexuality has appeared, the editorial evaluation escalates: "and God saw everything that [God] had made, and behold, it was *very* good" (Gen. 1:31, italics added).

So the later equation "sex=sin" did not enter Christian history from the Hebrew scriptures, where sex is viewed as a gift of God, but from the Greek culture in which the Christians found themselves, where a dualistic view, splitting soul from body, prevailed. If, as many Greeks maintained, the body is the prison house of the soul, then a low view of the body (and especially of its sexual functions) will naturally prevail, and the goal of salvation will be extrication from the evil body so that the pure soul can once again be free. (Many Christians unwittingly sustain this version of the Great Fallacy when they talk about eternal life exclusively in the imagery of "the immortality of the soul". This view increasingly dominated Christian thinking, displacing the inherited Jewish view that the body is "the temple of the Lord" and therefore sacred rather than evil.

Augustine (AD 354–430) played a central role in the creation of this legacy. A talented philanderer before his conversion, Augustine had great difficulty getting his own sex life under control, a fact he was honest enough to acknowledge in the prayer "O God, give me chastity, but not yet." Once he had seen the light, however, Augustine developed a negative Christian ethic of sex with all the zeal of a true believer and bequeathed to the subsequent tradition a conviction that sin had entered into the human condition through the sexual union of Adam and Eve, not only causing their downfall but leaving all – repeat, all – of their descendants tainted with sin as a result. Sex was therefore an evil, even though a necessary evil, since the continuation of the human race depended on it. Augustine walked the tightrope of this dilemma by concluding (a) that sex belonged only in marriage; (b) that it could be engaged in only for the purpose of having children; and (c) that it was to be tolerated under conditions (a) and (b) only so long as the partners got no enjoyment from it. Married people populate earth, he grudgingly conceded, but virgins populate heaven.

Building on such conclusions, the church decreed that one of the signs of true sanctity was virginity, and that all who were set apart for priestly functions must be celibate – one of the less popular decisions in the two thousand years of Christian history. In the resulting male-dominated church, women (unless they entered holy orders and took vows of celibacy themselves) were looked upon not only as unclean but as sources of temptation. The demeaning of sex carried with it the demeaning of women, and Christian literature is full of put-downs of the seductiveness of feminine charm, warnings about the carnal desires that women arouse in men, and the exclusion of women from roles of leadership in the church. This demeaning persists in Roman Catholicism today, where women are still excluded from leadership roles, where teaching about sex reiterates that the chief function of intercourse is procreation, and where artificial means of birth control, making marital sex possible for mutual enrichment as well as procreation, are forbidden.

This baleful history is an example of the Great Fallacy writ large. Had the Jewish-biblical view prevailed, the goodness of all that is earthy, immediate and sexual would not have been downplayed for so many centuries.

Spirituality and sexuality intermingled: a longer history

What is therefore needed is a rejection of this view and the recovery of an understanding of the unity of the human person – frequently described as a "psychosomatic" understanding. Etymology can help us with this difficult but important word. The Greek words *psyche* and *soma* mean, respectively, "soul" and "body". When we put them together they become *psychesoma* ("soulbody"), from which we get our transliteration "psychosomatic". It is significant that this is one word rather than two, for it underlines the fact that there is a unity rather than a duality to the human person. We are not talking about a good soul trapped in an evil body, but about a total being who can do many different things – think, fight, remember, love, anticipate, pray, copulate, sing, laugh, imagine. *All* the activities can be used for good ends, all can be abused and turned to evil ends.

This suggests that spirituality and sexuality, rather than being understood as opposites, should be understood as intimately and inextricably bound together, two expressions of a single basic reality rather than two different realities.

In the light of this, let us take a second look at the "tampering" that was done to the Song of Songs, the Jewish canticle to sensual human love. Christians, as we have seen, tried to allegorize the poem by transforming the images describing the love of two human beings for each other into images of the love of Christ for the church. What the original authors saw as good, Christians saw as prurient, and so they tried to exclude sex from the purview of their highly susceptible readers.

Suppose, however, that we let the analogy of the Christian redactors stand for the moment, not because, like them, we wish to deny the reality of sex but because, unlike them, we wish to celebrate and affirm it. In that case, we would be saying one of two things or, better still, both of them. We would be saying, first:

> If we want an image for the highest love of all, God's love for us (in this case, Christ's love for the church), then the best image we can employ is an image of the highest love we can know in human terms, the love of human beings for each other.

Or we would be saying, secondly:

> If we want an image for the highest love that human beings can have for one another, then the best image we can employ is an image of the highest love of all, God's love for us (in this case, Christ's love for the church).

Or finally, if we were to try to say both things simultaneously, we would be saying:

> We cannot make a clear-cut distinction between God's love for us and our love for one another. While they are obviously not totally alike, they are so much more alike than they are unlike that reference to either will cast light on the other. We understand divine love better by reference to human love, and we understand human love better by reference to divine love.

In coming to such conclusions we would not be doing violence to other parts of the biblical tradition but exemplifying them. The place where this is seen most clearly is in the story of the prophet Hosea. On first reading, there seem to be two stories in Hosea: the story of Hosea's love for his wife, and the story of God's love for Israel. But they are actually one overall story, in which each part is needed in order to understand the other.

The Hosea part of the story goes like this: Hosea falls in love with Gomer; they marry and have three children. Gomer becomes a prostitute. Hosea is directed by law and custom to throw her out of the household and make a public spectacle of her. But almost in the moment of doing so, he makes the astonishing discovery that he still loves her, despite all that has happened, and keeps her as his wife. The relationship is restored.

The God part of the story goes like this: God loves Israel and enters into a relationship with her called a covenant, that lasts many years. But Israel, too, becomes a prostitute – in the pungent language of the Authorized Version she goes a-whoring after false gods – the idols, the Baalim, of the fertility cults. God, by the terms of their agreement, is entitled to throw Israel on the scrap heap, and there are moments when the divine anger is so kindled that that seems likely to be the result (see Hos. 6:5–7, for example). But then comes the astonishing discovery that the divine love cannot be quenched. Despite all that has happened God still loves Israel and cannot cast her out. The relationship is restored (see Hos. 11:8–11).

Question: Did Hosea have his own experience of ongoing love in spite of betrayal, and then decide that if he could love Gomer despite her unfaithfulness, so could God love Israel despite *her* unfaithfulness? Or did Hosea, aware of God's ongoing love for Israel despite Israel's infidelities, decide, when faced with a parallel situation in his own life, that he should emulate God's ongoing love for Israel by his own ongoing love for Gomer?

Answer: (a) We don't know for sure and (b) it doesn't really matter.

What does matter is that the author of the book of Hosea intuited a deep truth: that love between two persons and love between God and persons are so much alike that they can be thought of almost interchangeably. There are more similarities than dissimilarities. The result is that the experience of human love helps us understand divine love, and the experience of divine love helps us understand human love. Each illumines the other. Neither is really full or true without the other.

Spirituality and sexuality revisited: an updated history

So far the biblical story. But for many people today the biblical story doesn't work any more. It seems offensive because it is based on stereotype sex roles: man as the aggrieved partner who has been wounded by his wife's infidelity; woman as the seductress who takes on other lovers and flaunts those relationships before her husband. How can anyone today learn from such an askew scenario?

Let us accept the legitimacy of the grievance. Could we tell the story of Hosea in modern dress by reversing the sex roles? Without attributing any such intention to her, we can see enough of the Hosea story in Nora Ephron's novel *Heartburn* to make the experiment worth trying. In her version contemporary counterparts of Hosea and Gomer are married and have children, and then Hosea enters into a long-standing affair with one of Gomer's best friends, which, it turns out, is only the most recent in a series of long-standing affairs and one-night stands. Gomer, appropriately indignant, leaves Hosea and holds him up to public ridicule by writing a novel that is only a thinly veiled account of the whole story. The account ends as Gomer, with exquisite marksmanship, throws a pie that hits Hosea in the face during a public banquet.

Of course, if this modern story was a consistent retelling of the biblical story, the account would not end there. Gomer would discover that she still loves Hosea despite his long string of infidelities, and out of her valid anger in the pie-throwing episode she would move to forgiveness, and after some transforming work on both sides the relationship would be restored.

One can imagine the furore that might have resulted had Nora Ephron employed such a twist of plot. Her book would have been described as one more instance of how men have their cake and eat it too, in a male-dominated world where women (the "weaker sex") crawl back, almost asking for further humiliation.

Fair enough. But the retort helpfully clarifies something else that is going on in the biblical version. For if our modern Gomer would be seen as spinelessly capitulating to a wily male, so much the more would the biblical Hosea have seemed craven and weak in terms of the expectancies of his time – a time when men were not supposed to be manipulated by fallen women but were expected to dominate and control them with all the appropriate macho and Rambo-like responses. Hosea defied all that when he took Gomer back, breaking with custom for the sake of love.

The point of the story survives, whether it is the woman who stumbles and the man who picks her up or the man who has the roving eye and the woman who restores his vision. In either case, compassion is operative. Human love is not evil; it is where we gain our knowledge of God's love.

Kierkegaard fumbles and Buber recovers: a recent history

This is even clearer in the contrasting attitudes towards the relationship of human love and God's love in the thought of Søren Kierkegaard, a nineteenth-century Danish theologian, and Martin Buber, a twentieth-century Jewish philosopher.

Kierkegaard, who wanted to give himself unreservedly to the love of God, wooed a young girl, Regina Olsen, for several years before finally prevailing upon her to say yes. No sooner had she done so, however, than Kierkegaard had second thoughts and decided that to marry Regina would distract him from loving God unreservedly. Out of loyalty to what he considered a "higher" love, he decided to relinquish the "lower" one. "In order to come to love [of God]," he wrote, "I had to remove the object [that is, Regina]."

Martin Buber comments on Kierkegaard's decision in a marvellous way:

> That is sublimely to misunderstand God. Creation is not a hurdle on the road to God, it is the road itself. We are created along with one another and directed to a life with one another. Creatures are placed in my way so that I, their fellow-creature, by means of them and with them, find the way to God. A God reached by their exclusion would not be the God of all lives in whom all life is fulfilled . . . *God wants us to come to [God] by means of the Reginas [God] has created, and not by renunciation of them.* (*Between Man and Man*, p. 52, italics added; New York, Macmillan, 1965)

Buber's words are appropriate not only in response to Kierkegaard but in response to all attempts to sever love of God and love of creatures. Bianco da Siena (c. 1367) would have merited a similar response. Writing about the Holy Spirit, she prays, movingly,

> O Comforter, draw near,
> Within my heart appear,
> And kindle it,
> Thy holy flame bestowing,

words that are unexceptional, save that she then goes on:

> O let it freely burn,
> Till earthly passions turn
> To dust and ashes
> In its heat consuming.

That, too, "is sublimely to misunderstand God".

Martin Buber is widely known for reflections on what he

calls an "I–Thou" relationship between two human beings, in which each treats the other as a subject with whom there can be full reciprocity and sharing, in contrast to an "I–It" relationship, in which the other is reduced to an "object" (as Kierkegaard described Regina) who can be manipulated and used and is thus depersonalized from a "thou" to an "it". So much is well known. What is less well known, but equally important, is Buber's claim that any real "I–Thou" relationship points to, and is grounded in, the Eternal Thou. Truly to enter into relationship with another human being is to enter into relationship with God. From this perspective also, we are to come to God by means of the Reginas and not by renunciation of them.

But before we erase all distinctions, we need to remember Dietrich Bonhoeffer's blunt statement that for a man to be thinking about God while embracing his wife is, to say the least, in bad taste – a sentiment with which the wife might be inclined to agree. If we so fully equate love of God and love of a human partner that when we love the human partner we are thinking only of God, we are dangerously damaging both relationships. No person, after all, wants to be loved merely as a symbol of something else; we want to be loved for who we are, with our distinctive strengths and weaknesses.

It is seldom the case, however, that we obliterate the presence of the one we are embracing and experience the occasion as nothing but a time of the presence of God. We are more likely to be so enchanted by the immediacy of the human love that God comes in a distant second. Yet even so, the paradox remains that in the midst of passionate sexual embrace, that very "I–Thou" relationship is also rooted in God, whether or not God's reality is consciously acknowledged by the lovers.

It might seem from the above that the only location for recognizing the interrelatedness of divine and human love is heterosexual marriage, and it is true that in Christian theology this has been a consistent theme. But it is also true in human experience that relationships between two women, or between two men, or between men and women not married to one another have been channels of divine grace, and the same thing can be said for relationships in which age or physical impairment have made sexual relations impossible.

Many issues are raised here that are beyond the scope of this particular book; the point at issue is simply that we cannot arbitrarily create boundaries around the ways God's love and human love can intersect.

"Where love is, there God is": an enduring history

There is no formula to which all these matters can be reduced, but we can begin to realize that the co-mingling of divine and human love is more possible than we had imagined. The presence of the Eternal Thou can enrich our relationship to a human thou, as Buber promised, and invest immediate moments and enduring relationships with new depth. If *eros* (in which the other is attractive and desirable to us) is the basic stuff of human relationships, it is still true that *agape* (love offered without counting the cost) is crucial if the relationship is to deepen. Lynn Rhodes helpfully expresses the intermingling of spirituality and sexuality:

> Our love is embodied in our feelings, our touch, our passion and our care. If spirituality loses touch with its roots in sexuality, it loses power to form and inform our deepest selves. When sexuality is separated from spiritual development, it becomes something we use to manipulate, control, and harm what we profess to love. When spirituality is separated from our sexuality, it loses the power of personal connection and becomes lifeless – it cannot move us to passionate care for this world. (Rhodes, *Co-Creating: a feminist vision of ministry*, pp. 64–5. Philadelphia, Westminster Press, 1987)

A musical refrain from the liturgy of the Taizé Community in southern France reinforces the point:

Ubi caritas
et amor,
ubi caritas
Deus ibi est.

We can translate this roughly as "Where there is love, God is present" or (using the title of a short story by Tolstoi), "Where love is, there God is also." The refrain reminds us that there can be no final separation between God's love and human love, since love constitutes the deepest possible sharing between persons, and shared loved constitutes the very nature of God. When love is present, God and persons meet; the Eternal Thou is there.

The insight did not originate at Taizé. The First Letter of John says it best: "Beloved, let us love one another; for love is of God, and the one who loves is born of God and knows God. Those who do not love do not know God; for God is love" (1 John 4:7–8, adapted). The author is not talking only of sexual love, but he is not excluding it either. Just as love of God is expressed in love for human beings, so love of human beings expresses love of God. To be dazzled by the fact that another person loves us, when there are so many good reasons not to, is to experience the quality of divine love, since it too is a gift, similarly undeserved and yet given anyhow. Divine love and human love do not work at cross-purposes; they are reminders of the sheer wonder and unity of our existence.

PART III
Radical Reconstruction

WHEREIN *it is shown that a "radical" approach to spirituality and liberation, discovering the "root" of their various meanings, establishes that each, truly understood, includes what is meant by the other*

WHEREIN *some of the implications of this conclusion for both our acting and our speaking are explored*

AND WHEREIN *finally, recognizing the danger of cerebral solutions, we observe a variety of persons and events, which, taken together, validate the equivalency of spirituality and liberation more convincingly than any book can do*

8

Plan C: an exercise in redefinition

If I am hungry, that is a physical problem; if my neighbour is hungry, that is a spiritual problem.

Nicolai Berdyaev, who, without quite escaping the vocabulary of the Great Fallacy, is still on the right track

In our age, the road to holiness passes through the world of action.

Dag Hammarskjöld, General Secretary of the United Nations

There are few words more dangerous than "spiritual".
George McLeod, founder of the Iona Community

Twin dangers and the need for a radical approach

George McLeod is right, in two very different ways. First of all, a superficial understanding of the word "spiritual" that equates it with otherworldliness is indeed dangerous. It allows us either to dismiss the notion of spirituality as irrelevant to our immediate lives, or to attach so much importance to it that it pre-empts the legitimate attention we ought to give to our immediate lives.

But "spiritual" can have other meanings than superficial ones – meanings that render it "dangerous" in more significant ways. For if we understand "spiritual" in its deepest sense we find that it calls upon us to take risks, to change our priorities, to surrender our sense of self-importance, to be more concerned with the doing of God's will than our own will, and many other things that are inconvenient and dangerous to well-ordered lives.

Going George McLeod one better, we could also argue that "there are few words more dangerous than 'liberation'". First of all, a superficial understanding of the word "liberation" that equates it with the-violent-overthrow-of-existing-governments-by-those-who-give-covert-allegiance-to-Marx-while-overtly-mouthing-Christian-platitudes is "dangerous". It allows us to dismiss the notion of liberation as irrelevant to our immediate lives, since such proposals strike us as preposterous, or to attach so much importance to bringing about social change that we justify all moral excesses in reaching that goal.

But "liberation" can have other meanings than superficial ones – meanings that render it "dangerous" in more significant ways. For if we understand "liberation" in its deepest sense, we find that it calls upon us to take risks, to change our priorities, to surrender our sense of self-importance, to be more concerned with the doing of God's will than with our own will, and many other things that are inconvenient and dangerous to well-ordered lives.

The preceding chapters have given us the tools to rise above superficial understandings and look for root meanings that will demonstrate that spirituality and liberation are finally two ways of talking about the same thing, as the repetitive style of the above four paragraphs has tried to suggest.

This demands a "radical" approach that we will call Plan C. And the introduction of such an adjective demands an explanation.

The words "spirituality" and "liberation" are so difficult in themselves that proposing to clarify them by using an even more difficult word, "radical", seems a perverse route to illumination. But the proposal of a "radical" approach is a serious one that can shed new light on our terms.

In political life "radical" is often used pejoratively, equated with "leftist", describing someone who favours basic change in our sociopolitical-economic structures. From such a perspective "liberals" are bad enough, sniffing the seductive scent of socialism, but "radicals" are worse, since they are either very smart (covering up their real aims with diversionary rhetoric) or very stupid (letting themselves be "used" by Communists who exploit their naivety for nefarious ends). This is not the primary sense in which "radical" will be used in the following pages, although we will discover some important political implications before we are through.

The Latin word *radix, radicus* (from which we get "radical") means "root". A radical approach, then, is one that tries to get at the root of things, to dig beneath the surface and discover what is really going on. The dictionary defines it as "going to the foundation or source of something", to what is fundamental or basic. The antonym, or opposite, of "radical" is "superficial" or "shallow". (Peter DeVries describes one of his characters with the words, "Oh, on the surface he's profound, but way down deep he's shallow.")

A description of "radical" from the field of chemistry offers further help: "A group of two or more atoms that acts as a single atom and goes through a reaction unchallenged, or is replaced by a single atom; it is normally incapable of separate existence." Spirituality and liberation sometimes appear to be "two atoms"; in the full understanding towards which we are pressing, however, they are replaced by a single atom and are "incapable of separate existence".

A "radical" approach then, is dissatisfied with surface impressions and tries to get at the heart of the matter, whether the object of scrutiny is the Holy Roman Empire, the *Tractatus* of Wittgenstein, the "spirit" of the Renaissance, the non-negotiable demands of a terrorist, or the meaning of spirituality and liberation. And in the last case we find that when we do get to the root meaning of either term, *the inclusive reality to which each of them points is the same reality.*

The new saints

Let us begin the exercise of redefinition by looking at popular piety in Latin America – a more faithful index than academic treatises – where we discover a new understanding of spirituality emerging. For centuries it was the custom to look for the "saints" among those who disengaged from the world and sought to contemplate the divine in far-off places, whether desert, monastery or convent. God was not found in the marketplace; God was as far from the marketplace as possible.

But Latin Americans are beginning to see that the true saints are not those who forsake the world but those who embrace it, involving themselves fully in its ambiguities, power struggles and trials.

Today the model for sainthood is someone like Archbishop Oscar Romero of El Salvador who, in the midst of the political corruption, sadistic violence and economic exploitation in his own country, did not ignore such realities or make his peace with them, but challenged them directly in the name of a Lord who likewise lived in the midst of political corruption, sadistic violence and economic exploitation and challenged them directly. No other posture was possible for Romero, once he saw that the God he served was the God who had taken the side of the exploited Israelites in Egypt and had later entered into the plight of those same oppressed people by sharing their humanity in Jesus of Nazareth, struggling at their side. He realized that only by a similar identification on his part, likewise at risk of death, could the liberating and resurrecting power of God be released in El Salvador.

In the case of both Jesus of Nazareth and Oscar of San Salvador, the attempt to show the indissolubility of liberation and spirituality led to death. Nothing could be more potently symbolic than the fact that Archbishop Romero was gunned down while saying mass. In the crucifixion of Jesus that the mass re-enacts, God chose to side with the victim rather than the apparent victors. The one whom God vindicated was not Pilate or Herod but Jesus, and his resurrection attested to the ultimate triumph of God over all that political and economic exploitation could attempt. As in first-century Jerusalem, so in twentieth-century San Salvador, Archbishop Romero affirmed with his words, his life and his death that the engagement of God in human lives is for the sake of their total healing, a redemption his detractors could neither measure nor control. "If I die," he said only weeks before his death in 1980, "I will rise again in the Salvadoran people."

He has.

The same can be said for three Roman Catholic sisters and a lay missionary – Dorothy Kazel, Ita Ford, Maura Clarke, and Jean Donovan – who likewise gave their lives in El Salvador in 1980. Their commitment to the "religious" life led to their increasing identification with poor and starving people, especially children. For working with "the least of these", for actions with and on behalf of the truly needy, for demonstrating that spirituality and liberation are inseparable, they were ambushed, assaulted, shot and left in an unmarked grave.

Those in political power could not accept the notion that such lives were authentic. Alexander Haig, then Secretary of State, fabricated a story about the nuns being gunrunners. Jeane Kirkpatrick, then US Ambassador to the United Nations, as much as said that the women got what they deserved. Ernest Lefever, Reagan's rejected nominee for Under Secretary of State, suggested that the four women had violated the meaning of a religious calling by becoming political.

Such rhetoric not only represents a frantic defence of the Great Fallacy in the corridors of power but is also a left-handed tribute to the integrity of Dorothy Kazel, Ita Ford, Maura Clarke and Jean Donovan, who in responding to the call of Christ were led not away from, but into the midst of, human need. In El Salvador (and also, alas, in Washington), siding with the poor is perceived as politically threatening and worthy of death.

The awesome truth is that for every archbishop, every sister, every lay missionary whose story is known, there are thousands of nameless ones – the new saints who embody the biblical truth that to know God is to do justice (Jer. 22:12–17). They demonstrate that eating and drinking, helping others get enough to eat and drink, struggling for justice, and discovering God in the midst of that struggle cannot be separated.

So a new kind of spiritual exercise is emerging. It involves not withdrawal but engagement; not shutting one's eyes to evil but opening one's eyes clearly to see both the individual and systemic reasons for that evil; not emptying the mind, so that the Spirit can flood into the emptiness, but filling the mind with statistics about who doesn't eat and why not, about where concentrations of wealth (and consequent injustice) are located, about indignities suffered by powerless people, so that the Spirit can be well informed in using the new saints in subsequent assaults on centres of exploitation and unjust privilege.

Meister Eckhart, many centuries ago, knew where the saints should be found. Reflecting on the fact that Paul was once lifted to "the third heaven", he continued: "Even if a man were in rapture like St Paul and knew of a man who was in need of food he would do better by feeding him than by remaining in ecstasy" (cited in O'Connor, *Search for Silence*, p. 118). Today we would also feel it important to help the man find a job. But Meister Eckhart is pointing in the right direction.

Redefining spirituality

Spirituality when radically understood includes what is meant by liberation. Recent discussions of spirituality almost always deny that it can be understood in an otherworldly or individual sense. Suppose we were to eavesdrop on a conversation about the meaning of spirituality today, undertaken by those who do not simply speak but embody that of which they speak. There would be some recurring themes:

The participants would insist that *spirituality includes all of life*. It would describe the way in which Christians live every aspect of their existence, including politics and merchandizing as well as prayer and meditation. The fullness of reality would be the reference point, not some isolated aspect of reality. The word "holistic" would figure in the discussion; perhaps John Carmody (author of *Holistic Spirituality*) would remind the others that all the domains of human existence – ecology, economics, health, prayer, politics, sexuality and education – are in the province of spirituality.

Before long someone in the group, perhaps a Latin American priest named Segundo Galilea, would spell this out as involving *simultaneous commitment to God and to persons*. From his perspective "contemplation would mean that personal encounter with Christ and personal encounter with our neighbour are inseparable". Others would add that our "neighbour" is anyone in need, particularly the poor and oppressed, and a biblical scholar such as Elsa Tamez from Costa Rica might add that the kingdom of God would be realized to just the degree that such concerns as justice and equality were the fruits of this "simultaneous commitment to God and to persons".

If the discussion began to get too complex Frei Betto, a Brazilian priest, might offer a disarmingly simple definition of spirituality, as no more and no less than *following Jesus*. Soon, however, what seemed disarmingly simple would begin to appear disconcertingly demanding, for it would become clear that just as Jesus became involved in historical conflict, so too would those who were "following" him be expected to do likewise. It would not be sufficient to follow Jesus only to quiet places such as deserts and mountain tops; he had a consistent pattern of going from such places into situations of turmoil. Placid serenity would not be the hallmark of such spirituality. Jesus would be seen as the "dangerous liberator" he was, more dangerous by far than the criminal Barabbas – a fact of which Pontius Pilate, the Roman procurator, was well aware.

Another voice, perhaps that of Jon Sobrino from El Salvador, would press the difference between "imitating" Jesus and "following" Jesus, insisting that since for Thomas à Kempis (as we have seen) *The Imitation of Christ* meant *Contempt for the World*, following Jesus must involve affirmation of the world as the arena in which he is to be followed, since the world is the place in which he decided, in love, to cast his own lot. "Christian existence," Sobrino would insist, "is the following of Jesus in a concrete situation" (*Christology at the Crossroads*, p. 395).

And on that note of specificity, someone would observe that the argument had come full circle, since (point one) "spirituality includes all of life" and "following Jesus" has now been shown to mean following him in "all of life". One of the participants might tie this together by recalling the statement made at a meeting of third world Christians in Brazil, that "in the following of Jesus the spiritual experience is never separated from the liberating struggle", and another would point out that the argument at the meetings had been capped by the subsequent assertion that "prayer and commitment are not alternative practices; they require and mutually reinforce one another. In the spirituality that we want to create, the option in solidarity with the poor and the oppressed becomes an experience of the God of Jesus Christ" (in International Ecumenical Congress of Theology, *The Challenge of Basic Christian Communities*, p. 240).

By this time there would be stirrings in the group to summarize their newly forged understanding of spirituality, and their attention would gradually focus on one of their number, Gustavo Gutiérrez, a Peruvian "liberation theologian" who had recently concluded just such an effort in a book called *We Drink from Our Own Wells: the spiritual journey of a people*. He would finally be prevailed upon to summarize his summary.

He would begin by reminding them and us that his title comes from a comment of Bernard of Clairvaux, that the place from which our spiritual nourishment comes is the place where we think, pray, and work; we begin our spiritual journey where we are, and not somewhere else. If the Latin Americans' "own wells" are located within the liberation struggle to which they are committed, our North American wells will likewise be found in our own situation, as we struggle, for example, with the affluence we so often use exploitatively. In either case, the life of spirituality will be located in the midst of the world's turmoil, rather than in safe havens of disengagement.

This cannot be done, Gutiérrez would continue, with an individualistic spirituality, and he would call attention to the important subtitle of his book, *the spiritual journey of a people*, as a reminder that spirituality must be communal. To show that this conviction is not idiosyncratic to himself, he might cite the comment of John de Gruchy from South Africa, another continent where oppression and struggle are daily companions of the Christian:

> The Christian life, while intensely personal, is always communal . . . The privatization of piety is not part of the Christian tradition and it undermines the Christian life . . . Christian spirituality is, therefore, the spirituality of Christian community. But it is not Christian community lived in isolation from the world. (De Gruchy, *Cry Justice*, p. 25)

Having rooted spirituality in the immediate human situation, Gutiérrez would then explore the riches of the biblical and historical traditions, in order to pave the way for five interconnected marks of the new spirituality of liberation. They are worth some attention, because they are as true for us in our situation as they are in his.

The first of these is *Conversion: a requirement for*

solidarity, and it involves a break with the past and the setting out on a new path that is both personal and social. Conversion involves both an acknowledgment of individual sin and a recognition that ours is a sinful situation containing structural causes of injustice. So conversion will involve the option to live in solidarity with those who attack sin on both levels. Hunger for God and hunger for bread go together.

A second characteristic is *Gratuitousness: the atmosphere for efficacy* (which we might render in less cumbersome fashion as "Grace: the basis for action"). God's gracious love is the source of everything else, including our own ability to love. Such love starts with the concrete need of the other, not with a "duty" to practise love. Drawing on Bernanos's theme that "all is grace", Gutiérrez reminds us that grace provides beauty for our lives, "without which even the struggle for justice would be crippled". Prayer expresses our faith and trust in the gracious God, a "living dialogue" that becomes a touchstone of life. There is always "a twofold movement": a full encounter with the neighbour presupposes the experience of grace, and Christ, as our way to God, is also our way to the neighbour.

The third note is *Joy: victory over suffering*. Gutiérrez does not gloss over the reality of suffering, but he also insists that the last word is "the joy born of the conviction that unjust mistreatment and suffering will be overcome". Such joy can be found even in a time of martyrdom, for to defend the poor easily leads to suffering and death. Martyrdom "is something that happens but is not sought" and Christians must never create a "cult of death". The only joy that can ultimately sustain us is "Easter joy", a joy that "springs from hope that death is not the final word of history". Those who encounter the cross are led to experience the resurrection.

The fourth mark is *Spiritual Childhood: a requirement for commitment to the poor*. The task, as Gutiérrez frequently remarks, is to be "with the poor and against poverty". The demands are severe: one must assume "voluntarily and lovingly the condition of the needy . . . in order to give testimony to the evil it represents". To do so will provoke opposition from the privileged, who are not enchanted when those within the church "disassociate themselves from the injustices of the prevailing system". Commitment to the poor means looking on the world of the poor "as a place of residence and not simply of work", sharing in exploitation, inadequate health care, and all the rest but also making new friends, experiencing a new kind of love, and developing "a new realization of the Lord's fidelity".

The fifth mark is *Community: out of solitude.* To be with the poor will mean going through "the dark night of injustice" oneself, enduring ostracism, fear, weariness, cowardice and despair, not to mention having to make crucial decisions when "nothing is clear". This is when we move "out of solitude" and into community. God does not call us to remain in the desert, but to pass through it on our way to the promised land. As we are drawn more deeply into community, we find foretastes of the promised land, even in the midst of the desert, places where the death and resurrection of Christ are remembered, and where the Eucharist becomes a point of departure and arrival. The mood is celebration.

> Spirituality [Gutiérrez concludes] is a community enterprise. It is a passage of a people through the solitude and dangers of the desert, as it carves out its own way in the following of Jesus Christ. This spiritual experience is the well from which we must drink. Through it we draw the promise of the resurrection.

Throughout Gutiérrez has been describing spirituality. Throughout Gutiérrez has been describing liberation.

Redefining liberation

Liberation when radically understood includes what is meant by spirituality. We can make our point by calling once again on Gutiérrez, who, as the practitioner of a life in which spirituality and liberation cannot be separated, has particularly compelling credentials. We need to call attention to only a single point made in his first major work, *A Theology of Liberation* (esp. pp. 36–7 and 176–81). If this point is clear, the case for the inclusiveness of spirituality and liberation has been established. It is Gutiérrez's contention that liberation has three levels of meaning but that none of them is properly understood unless all three are simultaneously affirmed.

The first level is *liberation from unjust social structures* that destroy people. These structures may be political, economic or cultural, they may grow out of warped attitudes based on race, class, nation or sex, and they may also (as Gutiérrez has personal reason to know) be embodied in church structures, operating in concert with any of the others. The attention of liberation theologians has been strongly focused on this level, since it is the most immediate barrier to full personhood that their constituencies face, and it has thrust many of them into conflictive situations.

The second level with which liberation is concerned is more subtle but equally devastating. It is *liberation from the power of fate*, from the sense that one's station in life is foreordained, and that not only is there nothing one can do about it but it would be presumptuous and arrogant even to try. If one is born poor, that is the way it is meant to be; if one is born rich, that too is the way it is meant to be. Good news to the rich, bad news to the poor. Result: apathy or despair among the poor and exhilaration among the rich who are determined to keep things that way. The counsel to accept whatever cards fate deals serves as a magnificent justification for the status quo, a fact not lost on the rich and powerful.

For hundreds of years the church played a major role in supporting this position, by the simple device of substituting "providence" or "the will of God" for the pagan concept of "fate". Accept your lot without complaint, the sermons went, and God will reward you in the afterlife.

The liberation message on this second level is that things need not remain the way they are, that the biblical God is working actively for justice and seeks to enlist all people in the struggle. The operative word is hope.

The third level of liberation is *liberation from personal sin and guilt.* This is not an add-on to the liberation agenda, inserted late in the day to forestall the critics, but has been there from the start, as any examination of the literature will show. Critics who fail to see it testify only to their own myopia. If the third level receives less quantitative treatment than the others, this is for the good reason that it has always been the central if not exclusive message of the institutional church, hardly in need of new champions, whereas levels one and two have only infrequently been acknowledged as part of the Christian agenda. Even so, the quantitative as well as qualitative attention given to such matters in Gutiérrez's writings is impressive. Prayer, Bible study, worship, Eucharist and (as we have seen) grace are central to his understanding of liberation.

The descriptions of the three levels thus far have been put in negative terms, as "liberation from . . ." But the positive counterparts are clear: liberation from unjust social structures means liberation *for* participation in creating a just society; liberation from fate means liberation *for* responsible action; liberation from sin and guilt means liberation *for* a grace-filled life, the "gratuitousness" of which Gutiérrez speaks so often.

The discussion is not complete without another reminder that we do not truly understand any of these levels unless we affirm them simultaneously. None has meaning without the other two. No liberation is "merely" political or "merely" biblical or "merely" anything else. It is all of them together:

> Our aspirations include not only liberation from *exterior* pressures which prevent our fulfillment as members of a certain social class, country, or society. We seek likewise an *interior* liberation, in an individual and intimate dimension; we seek liberation not only on a social plane but also on a psychological. (*A Theology of Liberation*, p. 30, slightly altered)

He quotes David Cooper approvingly: "If we are to talk of revolution today our talk will be meaningless unless we effect some union between the macro-social and the micro-social, and between 'inner reality' and 'outer reality'" (ibid p. 31).

And finally Gutiérrez again in a later work: "Liberation is an all-embracing process that leaves no dimension of life untouched" (*We Drink from Our Own Wells*, p. 2).

It should be clear that such comments do not mean a simplistic equating of the three levels of liberation. Gutiérrez reminds us that all three are necessary, but that they are not exactly the same: "one is not present without the other, but they are distinct" (*A Theology of Liberation*, p. 176). Otherwise we reduce the kingdom of God to nothing but a temporal process.

The interrelationship of the three levels of liberation recalls the interrelationship within Micah 6:8, a verse that, as we saw in Chapter 4, presents not three different exhortations but a single exhortation expressed in three different ways. Whether by fate, providence or sheer coincidence (let the reader decide), Micah's three variants happily coincide with the positive statements of Gutiérrez's three levels of liberation that we have just identified:

> to act justly = to participate in creating a just society
> to love tenderly = responsible action
> to walk humbly with God = a grace-filled life.

Throughout Gutiérrez has been describing liberation. Throughout Gutiérrez has been describing spirituality.

9

Plan C: some consequences

The affairs of the world, including economic ones, cannot be separated from the spiritual hunger of the human heart.

Roman Catholic bishops' pastoral letter
on the economy, para. 327

Holiness is not limited to the sanctuary or to moments of private prayer . . . holiness is achieved in the midst of the world.

The bishops again, para. 327

There is a spirituality that dares to sink roots in the soil of oppression-liberation.

Gustavo Gutiérrez,
We Drink from Our Own Wells

If that is all true, then at the very least we have to act differently and speak differently.

Towards a new way of acting

To Juan Luis Segundo, a Jesuit from Uruguay, the starting point for a liberating spirituality, as we saw earlier, is very simple: *The world should not be the way it is*. If you are satisfied with the way the world is, if you feel morally at ease within it, Segundo tells us, you will never understand what we are about, for we are *not* satisfied with the way the world is, and we do *not* feel morally at ease within it.

We see too much misery, too much exploitation, too many children with bloated stomachs, too many wretched slums, too many parents unable to provide for their children, too many poor whose lives and deaths are determined by too few rich.

That must all be radically changed, Segundo would argue – at the roots. No tidying up around the edges will suffice. To feed the poor a nourishing breakfast does not deal with the fact that they will be hungry again by supper time. Within the religious community too many people either come up with palliatives that do not basically change anything or assert that such problems are none of their business – a stance they justify by one version or another of the Great Fallacy.

Imagine, however, a group of people who are being forced to face such issues head on and whose reliance on the Great Fallacy is being exposed and discredited. Imagine that the relationship between how they worship God and how they deal with the world needs to be refocused, so that those two concerns become one. How will this change them? What will it do to their politics and to their worship?

Let us look at a typical "worshipping congregation" that has been living comfortably with the Great Fallacy and watch what happens when the divine boom is lowered. Happily there is a case study already at hand, thoughtfully provided by an unknown Hebrew prophet.

The backdrop of the passage (Isa. 58:1–12) is that God is highly displeased with the introspective character of the people's worship and instructs the prophet to make the divine displeasure clear beyond any shadow of a doubt: "Cry aloud, spare not, lift up your voice like a trumpet," and confront the people with their sins (v. 1). All the dirty laundry is to be hung out in full view of the neighbours.

This is a shock to the people, who had been under the impression that the newest liturgical detergent had left their religious practices gleaming. After all, they are part of a nation doing "righteousness" and following "the ordinance of their God" (v. 2). The code word in their culture for going the religious second mile is "fasting", a particular spiritual exercise that we can take as a symbol for *any* kind of worship or religious practice designed to curry favour with God.

So when the word of judgment comes in one of those prophetic trumpet blasts, they feel entitled to complain. They have been going out of their way to do the "extra" religious thing, and God hasn't even noticed how pious they are. In that case, why bother?

> Why have we fasted, and thou seest it not?
> Why have we humbled ourselves,
>   and thou takest no knowledge of it?
> (v. 3)

Ask a question, get an answer. When they fast, God responds, they only do it to get points for being pious. And not only that, but at the very moment they are preening themselves on their spiritual rectitude they are committing injustice in the workplace:

> Behold, in the day of your fast
> [in the midst of your religious practices]
> you seek your own pleasure,
>   *and oppress all your workers.*
> (v. 3, italics added)

If they ask another question, "But what has worship got to do with paying the minimum wage?" they will get another answer: everything. God will not even listen to people who make humble gestures, bow down their heads, and call that a sufficient exercise of their faith: "Fasting like yours this day will *not* make your voice heard on high" (v. 4, italics added). There is scorn as well as thunder in the divine voice:

> Will you call this a fast,
>   and a way acceptable to the LORD?
> (v. 5)

It's a rhetorical question.

By this time God has built up a considerable head of steam, and it is about to erupt. You want to know my idea of a fast, God continues, you want to know my idea of what is acceptable "worship"? I'll tell you. And God does, in one of the most powerful utterances in all scripture:

> Is not this the fast that I choose:
> to loose the bonds of wickedness,
> to undo the thongs of the yoke,
> to let the oppressed go free,
> and to break every yoke?
> Is it not to share your bread with the hungry,
> and bring the homeless poor into your house;
> when you see the naked, to cover [them],
> and not to hide yourself from your own flesh?
> (vv. 6–7)

And if that's still not clear, God continues, let me spell it out a little more, because you are going to have to make a choice:

> If you take away from the midst of you the yoke [of oppression], the pointing of the finger [of contempt], and speaking wickedness,
> if you pour yourself out for the hungry
> and satisfy the desire of the afflicted . . .
> (vv. 9–10)

. . . then things will be different, God promises, and a future full of hope can be anticipated – a future spelt out in glowing detail in the next verses.

Note well: *This exhortation to achieve justice in human relations is not part of the social action platform of the local synagogue but is a definition of worship.* This is the "fast", the kind of religious observance that God chooses, and its guiding principle is justice.

Our two apparently divergent definitions of "radical" (cited at the beginning of the last chapter) begin to overlap. For to worship "radically" (in the sense of getting to the root of what God asks of us) is to be thrust into a "radical" political stance (in the sense of working for basic change, rather than a cosmetic touching up of the way things are). We see this overlap clearly in the successive uses of the image of the "yoke" in the passage.

A yoke is worn by a beast of burden and indicates subservience to whoever is driving the beast, one who could well be a harsh taskmaster. To put a yoke on the neck of a person, as the Isaiah passage does, is to reduce that person to the level of a beast, to make that person subhuman. How is this situation to be overcome? The prophet outlines three steps, each more "radical" than its predecessor.

1 *To "undo the thongs of the yoke"* (v. 6): to loosen it, make it less painful, provide some immediate relief from the burden; in other words, to alleviate some of the immediate condition of social evil.
2 *To "break every yoke"* (v. 6), a more demanding challenge: to destroy the social structures symbolized by the yoke, whatever they are, that condemn people to live subhuman lives.
3 *To "take away from the midst of you the yoke"* (v. 9): not even to leave the debris around (that might tempt people to patch it up) but to banish the structures of oppression from the scene once and for all, repudiate them, so that they can never dominate again but can be replaced by structures patterned on justice rather than exploitation.

Not content simply to denounce, the prophet interlaces these comments with a suggestive laundry list of what the new structures will look like. True worship, the "true fast", will involve such things as:

1 The sharing of bread with the hungry, which in this new context will not simply mean making a few of our leftover slices available to those who don't have any, but working to create an economic order in which

everyone has direct access to bread and the money with which to pay for it.

2 Bringing the homeless poor into our houses, which will mean not only responding to the immediate situation of the tens of thousands of homeless people in our cities by providing shelter in our homes and churches and synagogues, but also working to create an economic order in which housing projects are built, and jobs provided, so that "the homeless poor" will have homes of their own to dwell in and will not be dependent on the charity of the affluent. In our day there must also be special action on behalf of the "homeless poor" from places like El Salvador and Guatemala, who have fled for their lives from death squads and whose ongoing survival depends on churches and synagogues providing "sanctuary" for them, so that the government is unable to deport them to likely death.

And the agenda continues throughout the passage: clothing the naked, being responsible to the members of one's own family, pouring ourselves out for the hungry, meeting the needs of the afflicted – all of which, by prophetic standards, will have to go far beyond charitable handouts and will involve new structures to replace the old.

Our starting point, provided by Fr Segundo, that "the world should not be the way it is", has led us in some surprising directions. Not only has it brought the two meanings of "radical" closer together, but it has indicated that our worship is defined by how we act for justice, and that how we act for justice defines our worship.

A new way of acting indeed.

Towards a new way of speaking

To the degree that we discover that spirituality and liberation are two ways of speaking about the same thing, we will discover that we need a new way of speaking, a new vocabulary. There will need to be some new words, not yet discovered, but in the meantime we can begin to invest some old words with new meaning.

Commenting on Gutiérrez's treatment of spirituality, for example, Henri Nouwen, a Dutch priest, shows that in reappropriating great themes from the past like conversion, gratuity, joy, spiritual childhood and community, Gutiérrez has given them new meaning for the present:

> These old words sound fresh and new when they have been distilled from the life experience of the suffering of the Latin American church. *Conversion* then emerges as part of a process of solidarity with the poor and the oppressed; *gratuity* as the climate of fruitful work for liberation; *joy* as victory over suffering; *spiritual childhood* as a condition of commitment to the poor; and *community* as a gift born out of the common experience of the dark night of injustice. (Foreword to *We Drink from Our Own Wells*, p. xix, italics added)

Tissa Balasuriya, a Sri Lankan priest, does much the same thing. In a chapter provocatively entitled "Towards a spirituality of justice", he takes the traditional notion of "prudence" (which has probably been employed to scuttle more movements for social justice than any other so-called Christian "virtue") and gives it revolutionary content:

> Prudence requires that we [do] not waste our time and energies in unnecessary battles and secondary issues, for this will dissipate the effort even of the well intentioned. Prudence will decide on the issues that are worth fighting for, as well as the means to be used in the struggle. Prudence tells us when it is necessary to bypass an issue and pursue it to the extent of polarization.
>
> Prudence will help us calculate risks so that risks taken will yield results. Prudence decides when to give oneself for a cause, even if it means such extreme sacrifices as imprisonment or life itself. The action of Che Guevara in joining the guerillas may have seemed imprudent in the short term. But in the long term it has made an inestimable contribution

> to the cause. A spirituality of liberation therefore involves an understanding of risk-bearing and disappointment. (Balasuriya, *Planetary Theology*, p. 265)

Johannes Metz, the European theologian most sensitive to third world views, has done a similar re-evaluation of the ascetic side of Christianity in the light of a "theology of the world". Metz sees asceticism, which has often been interpreted as a denial of the world, not as "flight from the world, but flight 'forward' with the world", an exercise in which another vision of what could be is juxtaposed to what is. Paul, for example "is critical not of solidarity with the world, but of conformism with it". Asceticism can thus have a "revolutionary quality, as protest against the present for the sake of the future".

From this perspective it is possible to assess mysticism in a new way, since it too has often been associated with "distance" from the world. In a paragraph that defies paraphase, Metz offers an illuminating corrective:

> Christian mysticism is neither a kind of pantheistic infinity mysticism, nor an esoteric mysticism of exaltation, tending toward the self-redemption of the individual soul. It is – putting it extremely – a mysticism of human bonding. But it does not proceed from an arbitrary denial of persons and the world, in order to seek to rise towards a direct nearness to God. For the God of Christian faith is found only in the movement of God's love towards persons, "the least", as has been revealed to us in Jesus Christ. Christian mysticism finds, therefore, that direct experience of God which it seeks, precisely in daring to imitate the unconditional involvement of the divine love for persons, in letting itself be drawn into the . . . descent of God's love to the least of God's brothers and sisters. Only in this movement do we find the supreme nearness, the supreme immediacy of God. And that is why mysticism, which seeks this nearness, has its place not outside, beside, or above responsibility for the world of our brothers and sisters, but in the centre of it. (Metz, *Theology of the World*, p. 104, slightly adapted)

New understandings of old words sneak up on us unawares. A commandment like "Thou shalt not steal" embodies conventional wisdom. It is invoked to ensure that I do not rob you. But since what is fair for one is fair for all, I insist on invoking it to ensure that you do not rob me – a reading that appeals to me tremendously, particularly as I am fortunate enough to accumulate more and more goods and thus need extra protection against your covetous eye. I, of course, have no interest in breaking into your modest dwelling for the sake of a few knickknacks, so I am no problem, but society needs a police force to keep watch over your proclivity to try shoplifting in my place of business.

However, if we take seriously the spirituality-liberation connection, we discover disturbing implications in this apparently straightforward commandment, that have been under wraps for centuries:

1 As far back as the early church fathers, it was noted that if I have more than I need, and you have less than you need, I am already committing "theft" against you and am breaking the commandment not to steal. John Chrysostom defines robbery as "not sharing one's resources", and Ambrose makes caustic remarks about situations in which "a naked man cries out, but you are busy considering what sort of marble you will have to cover your floors" and pay no heed. Theft.
2 Not only is the accusing finger being pointed at me, but you, as the one in need, are authorized to take from me what you need for your survival, no penalties incurred. In a remarkable passage in "The Church and the Modern World" the 2300 bishops at the Second Vatican Council stated:

> The right to have a share of earthly goods sufficient for oneself and one's family belongs to everyone . . . *If a person is in extreme necessity, such a one has the right to take from the riches of others what he or she needs.* (Para. 69, italics added)

3 Strictures against theft are targeted not only against individuals but against society. A society with a few wealthy and many poor is a thieving society, and those within it who benefit from such disparities are breaking the commandment "Thou shalt not steal". The remedy comes by appeals not only to individual behaviour but to responsible action on the part of society as a whole. The surprising bishops continue:

> According to their ability, let all individuals *and governments* undertake a genuine sharing of their goods. Let them use these goods especially to provide individuals and nations with the means for helping and developing themselves. (Para. 69, italics added)

In a recent work, *On Job: God-talk and the suffering of the innocent*, Gustavo Gutiérrez gives us further help on language by initially distinguishing two ways of talking about God in the book of Job.

Prophetic language stresses God's predilection for the poor. God loves the poor not because they are better than others but simply because they are poor. And this "preferential option for the poor" on God's part must be reflected in a similar "preferential option for the poor" on the part of those who worship God. God's grace and this preferential option go hand in hand.

Contemplative language is supported and reinforced by prophetic language. "Mystical language" (as Gutiérrez also calls it) "expresses the gratuitousness of God's love; prophetic language expresses the demands this love makes" (p. 95). Contemplative language acknowledges that everything comes from God's unmerited – that is, gracious – love. But the two languages are linked, as a passage in Jeremiah shows:

> Sing to the LORD;
>   praise the LORD!
> For [the Lord] has delivered the life of the needy
>   from the hand of evildoers.
>
> (Jer. 20:13)

The first two lines are contemplative, the latter two prophetic.

However, the point is not that "two languages – the prophetic and the contemplative – are required" but that "Both languages are necessary and therefore inseparable; they also feed and correct each other" (p. 95). But there is a further point – "they must also be combined and become increasingly integrated *into a single language*" (p. 94, italics added).

As Gutiérrez writes in an earlier essay:

> We need a language that is both contemplative and prophetic; contemplative because it ponders a God who is love; prophetic because it talks about a liberator God who rejects the situation of injustice in which the poor live, and also the structural causes of that situation. (in Fabella and Torres, eds, *Irruption of the Third World*, p. 232)

Without denying the importance of the words we speak directly to God in prayer, either in public or in private, we can begin to see from our new perspective how deeds themselves can be forms of prayer. A prayer of intercession may be a trip to the city jail to provide bail for someone wrongly arrested because of having the wrong skin colour; an act of praise of God may be the affirmation of a Laotian child's success in the English as a Second Language programme; an act of contrition may be persuading a Congressional representative to vote against aid to the Nicaraguan *contras*; a Hail Mary may be involvement in a political group trying to implement the concern for the poor that is celebrated in the Magnificat; a choral response may be joining in the cheers at a rally to reverse the arms race; a blessing may be the gift of time and money that enables a woman victimized by sexual harassment to secure legal help; a prayer of adoration may be the formation of a political coalition to fight a specific injustice.

Conversely, a word spoken to God in private may be the condition for a deed done for a victim in public; an inner impulse, empowered by grace, may generate a political conviction; a meditation on scripture may inspire an act of civil disobedience; hearing a sermon about Nathan challenging David may focus the need to challenge the Immigration Service or the State Department.

Laborare est orare – to work is to pray – was how the medieval monks put it. We are only beginning to catch up with them.

There is a trap into which we could fall, and it will take a final chapter to avoid it. The trap consists of implying that our discovery of the overlapping of spirituality and liberation is mainly a matter of the intellect.

Faithfulness to our subject matter compels us to acknowledge that this will not do. The recovery of the unity of spirituality and liberation must be exhibited in the day-to-day events of human lives rather than in the line-to-line sentences of human books.

We need not definitions but examples, not victories of logic but victories of love. And these are what we will seek in the final pages.

10

Showing by deeds what cannot be shown by words

Hope has two beautiful daughters. Their names are anger and courage: anger at the way things are, and courage to see that they do not remain the way they are.

Augustine

Whenever an angel says "Be not afraid!" you'd better start worrying. A big assignment is on the way.

Elie Wiesel, in conversation

Unfortunately no single word communicates the single reality we have identified. To write "spirituality/liberation" or "liberation/spirituality" works technically but remains awkward. Words already available carry enough accumulated baggage to invite misunderstanding. *Praxis* comes close, since it means the interrelationship of reflection and action, but it is so closely associated in our minds with "practice" that it is likely to distort as much as illuminate. *Shalom*, a beautiful Hebrew word, points to the wholeness of life, but it has been so widely employed as a synonym for "peace" that its meaning is too narrow for our purposes.

There is another way to communicate, however, that may be more faithful to our subject matter than seeking a new word. This is to use words that point not to definitions but to deeds – to episodes or persons or events that enact what our speech, by itself, cannot communicate.

There is good biblical precedent for this, most notably in the Letter to the Hebrews, where the unknown author is trying desperately to communicate something of the meaning of the word "faith". Let us assume that the author is a woman. She tries her hand at a formal definition: "Now faith is the substance of things hoped for, the evidence of things not seen" (Heb. 11:1 AV). Pretty abstract. She offers a historical generalization: "For by it [those] of old received divine approval" (v. 2). Not much better. Maybe cosmology will clarify: "By faith we understand that the world was created by the word of God" – her readers' faces are still blank. In desperation she turns to epistemology – "so that what is seen was made out of things which do not appear" (v. 3), a sentence destined to confuse rather than clarify.

By this time a gnawing question is working its way up into the author's consciousness: "Will this fly in Dubuque?" It is her considered – and correct – judgment that it will not. Dubuque couldn't care less.

Nothing to do, then, but start all over. First question: "How to explain faith?" Second question (which is an answer to the first question): "How about telling stories about people who exemplify faith, describing events in which faith is on the scene, lining up a cast of very different characters, ranging from harlots to heavenly beings, who have at least in common that faith is written all over who they are?"

It works. The next forty verses (spilling over into Chapter 12) are as exciting as the first four are dull. She calls up Abel, Noah, Abraham, Sarah, Rahab, Isaac and Joseph, among others, and one whom she describes as the "pioneer and perfecter" of the faith; she takes her readers on hikes through the wilderness; she lets them participate in crossing a body of water without getting wet; she describes battles and tumbling city walls, resurrections, torture scenes, duels – a vast historical kaleidoscope that replaces definitions with deeds.

Dubuque is listening.

We will take our cue from the author. Although we will not range as widely as she did, or assume that our efforts will one day be enshrined in Holy Scripture, we will likewise forsake further formal definition and offer a contemporary kaleidoscope of events distinguished by the fact that within them spirituality and liberation are cut from the same cloth. Using terminology from her letter, we will call it:

A cloud of witnesses

There is a Dutch priest named Henri Nouwen, and for many years Henri Nouwen has been "Mr Spirituality" – or, more properly, "Fr Spirituality" – not only to many Catholics but to many other Christians as well. They turn to him for devotional reading, for suggestions about what to do "on retreat", for help in deepening their prayer life. Through his writings and his person he is a tutor to the human spirit; in the realms of the personal, the individual, the inward, his role as a spiritual director is grace-filled and sustaining.

And then one day Henri Nouwen discovers that he must test a prompting that has come to him in his own devotional life. Perhaps he has a vocation to settle in Latin America and live among the poor, seeking to combine a life of prayer with a sharing in their ongoing struggle for justice.

As he goes to Latin America no lights flash and no bells ring, but he realizes immediately (as he records in his journal, *¡Gracias!*) that "Prayer and work with the poor belong together" (p. 10) and that the need to pray increases when people are confronted with oppression and exploitation. His reading of the Bible and his discernment of the contemporary world begin to inform one another: "I try to remember that Jesus was killed as a subversive . . . under the accusation of being an enemy of the ruling class" (p. 29). And again: "[The words of the Magnificat] today have taken on so much power and strength that, in a country like El Salvador, they are considered subversive and can be a cause of torture and death" (p. 68).

Events in the liturgical year take on new relevance in

the context of living among the poor. The feast of St John of the Cross, for example, reveals the intimate connection between resistance and contemplation: "[St John] reminds us that true resistance against the powers of destruction can only be a lifelong commitment when it is fed by an ardent love for the God of justice and peace" (p. 72).

Whatever the final outcome of Henri Nouwen's quest, he realizes that it is no longer possible to be a contemplative without taking political revolution into account, and that praying in the future may mean praying in the midst of a revolution rather than at a distance.

Henri Nouwen's new engagement in the struggle for social justice is an expression of his prayer life, not an alternative.

There is a splendid sign in the chapel of Temple Emmanuel Shalom in Burlingame, California, which in addition to the sign also contains a pulpit, an ark, the Torah and all the other normal accoutrements of Jewish worship. The sign is a public declaration from the local fire department indicating maximum legal occupancy under a variety of conditions.

The sign is interesting in that – like most such things – its message is unexpected. It does not stipulate "62 Persons for Prayer Services", "47 Persons for Bar Mitzvahs or Bat Mitzvahs" or other ceremonies usually associated with chapels. The sign simply says that the maximum legal occupancy in this place of worship is:

26 DINING
55 DANCING

There is a marvellous recognition that "earthy" things like having meals and throwing dances – celebratory events – are not only not excluded from places of worship but are expressions of what places of worship are for. How do we celebrate God's reality? Give a party!

Somebody has finally caught up with that curious passage in Exodus we have already noted: "They beheld God, and ate and drank" (Exod. 24:11).

Peggy Hutchison stands in the United States District Court in Tucson, Arizona, Judge Earl Carroll presiding, waiting to be sentenced. She has been found guilty of conspiracy in violation of Title 18, United States code 371. In less abstract language, she has been convicted of helping political refugees escape from death squads in El Salvador and Guatemala, so that they can find sanctuary in the United States until it is politically safe for them to go back home. Has she anything to say "by way of mitigating evidence" before sentence is imposed?

She has.

She tells the court that her family and the United Methodist Church both helped to shape her values and taught her that beliefs didn't mean anything unless she put them into action. Her church enjoined her in its Discipline to be part of "a witnessing and serving community". As she worked with political refugees on both sides of the border she soon realized, as she informed Judge Carroll, that "they have fled torture, they have fled imprisonment, civil war, and death", and that to turn her back on them would make her complicit in actions that would imperil them all over again.

She discovered by bitter experience that the immigration courts, the procedures of the Immigration and Naturalization Service, and the policies of the Border Patrol were conspiring to make it impossible for political refugees to escape deportation. She reminded the judge that the United States had reacted with similar callous disregard to the plight of Jews seeking to emigrate to the United States after the rise of Hitler, and that "never again" must that happen. She came to the conclusion that the immigration laws were not being fairly administered, and that the lives and deaths of people must be her paramount concern.

As she had said before the trial, her political involvement was heightened not just by her study of the law but by her study of scripture. Passages like "Do not mistreat foreigners who are living in your land . . . Love them as you love yourselves" (Lev. 19:33–4, adapted) jumped out at her. Jesus' admonitions, as she summarized them, to "feed the hungry, clothe the naked, welcome the stranger, take care of the sick, visit the imprisoned" (cf. Matt. 25:31–46), seemed to have been written for the precise situation in which she found herself, and they could not be ignored.

In the face of this conflict between human law and divine gospel, she reports that she "spent time in meditation, reflection, and prayer". Rather than providing relief from her political dilemma, the meditation, reflection, and prayer confronted her with a series of options, from within which she knew she had to choose: "I could collaborate with the United States government, which helps sponsor the torture of thousands of people; I could learn to live with atrocity; or I could stand with the oppressed and persecuted Salvadorans and Guatemalans and respond to these sojourners in my midst."

The consequence of making the latter choice not only heightened her political activity (until her arrest) but simultaneously deepened her faith – a not surprising consequence, since in her life "political activity" and "faith" are not two but one.

And there was a gift as well. She learned that the refugees to whom she was ministering were ministering in turn to her. It was from them, she reports, that she discovered how to live in the midst of exploitation, destruction and death and still affirm hope, resurrection, life . . . and change.

No one who tries to understand Peggy Hutchison's experience will be tempted to separate her life into a "spiritual" compartment and a "liberation" compartment.

No one perhaps, except a district court judge, who, after hearing the "mitigating evidence", sentenced her to five years probation.

Rabbi Abraham Joshua Heschel was a professor at the Jewish Theological Seminary in New York City until his death in 1972. He had come to the United States from his native Poland shortly before Hitler's forces invaded his homeland and destroyed all the Jews they could find.

One of the most remarkable things about Heschel's years at the Jewish Seminary was his title. He was not just an ordinary "professor"; he was – in a title that was a clear consequence of divine inspiration – Professor of Mysticism and Ethics.

Many people find mysticism a topic beyond their comprehension, and at least as many people, in this relativistic era, find ethics equally baffling. Join them – mysticism and ethics – suggesting that they belong together, and the mystery is compounded beyond apparent resolution. Hard enough to be a professor of either, but to be a professor of both?

Those who knew Heschel found nothing incongruous in the title. It was simply a description of who he was – never just the mystic, never just the ethicist, but an authentically integral human being in whom the two were one. He could write a beautiful book on the Sabbath and march in civil rights demonstrations at Selma, Alabama, saying, "Today we are praying with our feet." He could simultaneously inveigh against the immorality of the US action in Vietnam and invoke the mercy of God, whether in pulpit or public square. He could glory in the tasks of scholarship and give his energy to improving relations between blacks and Jews. He could meet with popes to alter the course of Jewish–Christian relationships and instruct young rabbis in Torah. The one whose presence could remind others of the majesty of the prophets, and of the God to whom the prophets witnessed, could also enjoy a good cigar.

In his later years Heschel formed an abiding friendship with the Protestant theologian Reinhold Niebuhr, a neighbour in New York City, of whom he wrote, in words that are a perfect description of Heschel as well:

> His spirituality combines heaven and earth . . . It does not separate soul from body, or mind from unity of our physical and spiritual life. His way is an example of one who does

> justly, loves mercy, and walks humbly with his God, an example of the unity of worship and living. (Heschel, *The Insecurity of Freedom*, p. 147)

Sometimes it takes one to know one.

It is my first communion service after ordination. It is taking place on the after gun turret of a US Navy destroyer during the Second World War, and I am there because I am a navy chaplain. There is only room for three communicants at a time to come forward and receive the elements. The first three to respond to the invitation are a lieutenant-commander, captain of the vessel; a fireman's apprentice, about as low as one can be in the ordinary naval hierarchy; and a steward's mate, who, because he is black, is not even included in the ordinary naval hierarchy; all blacks can do in the then Jim Crow navy is wait on the tables where the white officers eat.

An officer, a white enlisted man, a black enlisted man – day by day they eat in separate mess halls. There are no circumstances in which they could eat together at a navy table. But at the Lord's table, not even navy regulations can dictate who eats with whom. For this one moment – as is true during no other moments on shipboard – they are equals, and they are at the same table. Here is the one place where hierarchical statutes do not prevail. To make the point, I serve the black enlisted man first, the enlisted man second, the commanding officer last.

Holy Communion is usually described as the highest "spiritual" experience Christians can have. That particular Holy Communion was a "liberation" experience as well – liberation for a moment from the structures that otherwise separated those three men, and a liberation enacting in advance the kind of new structures that would someday prevail even in the US Navy.

Spirituality, liberation. No separation.

Many communions later I am helping to celebrate at the General Assembly of the Presbyterian Church of Southern Africa in the city of Durban. The black and white members of that denomination worship separately for fifty-one Sundays a year. During the week of General Assembly, however, they meet together, study together, eat together, worship together.

We distribute bread and wine to the deacons, who will partake before serving the congregation. They are lined up before the Lord's table – black, white, black, white, white, black, white, black, black, white – a random selection. The bread is passed from hand to hand, and each hand, whether black or white, breaks off a piece to give to his or her neighbour. No hesitation. No problem.

And then a common cup – a single chalice – is passed down the line, lifted first to black lips, then to white lips, then to black lips. No hesitation. No problem.

I, a visitor to that land, would not have believed it possible. The "spiritual" act of sharing the body and blood of Christ becomes an occasion of "liberation" for all those people – liberation for a moment from bondage to the fierce laws that on all other occasions legislate the separate sharing of food and drink by black and white. One day the fierce laws will change and the exception, enacted in that service, will be the rule. Much more blood – Christ's blood in Christ's children, both black and white – will be shed before the day when it is so, and that is a great tragedy. But it *will* come, in part because the distance between Christ's table and all other tables can no longer be tolerated, and that is a great hope.

Spirituality, liberation. No separation.

The steps of the Federal Building, San Francisco, December 4, 1967. The occasion: a draft card turn-in by young men who are declaring that they will not fight in an immoral war. A political act. And an act of worship.

Each participant comes forward and places his draft card in the offering plate, symbolizing the offering of himself to oppose the killing. The cards are then lifted up – eighty-seven that day, as it turns out – blessed, placed in a large envelope addressed to the Office of Selective Service in Washington, and mailed by the participating clergy, who, in "aiding, counselling and abetting" the draft resisters, place themselves in the same legal jeopardy as their younger compatriots.

When those cards were first mailed to their original addresses, they were messengers of *death*, summoning the addressees to participate in killing Vietnamese peasants. In the liturgical act of their gathering and remailing, they are transformed into messengers of *life*, declaring that their former owners are unwilling, no matter what the cost or inconvenience, to enlist in the service of death. Outwardly the cards have not changed; inwardly they are totally changed – from messengers of death to messengers of life.

I reflect that this is about as close as I, a Protestant, will ever come to understanding the ancient doctrine of transubstantiation – the belief that in the Roman mass the bread and wine, while outwardly unchanged, become, after the words of consecration, the actual body and blood of Christ.

On the steps of the Federal Building in San Francisco a "spiritual" experience of common worship is an act of "liberation" for eighty-seven young men, freed from bondage to the powers of death, freed for a future in which they can "choose life, so that they and their descendants may live".

Spirituality, liberation. No separation.

Members of the Iona Community, a movement for reform within the Church of Scotland, believe (as we have previously suggested) that "liturgy" is *all* the work we do, both inside and outside the church. They have developed a daily way of issuing this reminder.

When they gather each morning for worship they engage in a fairly conventional service, with scripture, hymns and prayers, but the service ends unconventionally; there is no "benediction", no conclusion. Instead they go directly from the chapel to whatever tasks they will be doing that day – helping to build a new dormitory, baking bread in the kitchen, mixing cement, rounding up cattle that have got loose. That is their continuing "liturgy", their work, until it is time to return to the chapel in the evening. Once again they engage in a fairly conventional service, with scripture, hymns and prayers, but the service starts unconventionally; there is no "call to worship", no beginning, since they have been "at worship" all day long and what is happening now is simply a continuation of that worship in another form. The whole day is their "liturgy"; their work in church and their work outside are interconnected varieties of the one work. Only at the very end of the full day, when all the tasks are completed, is there a "benediction", a blessing for the day and a prayer for rest during the night.

Latin America is a land of martyrs, famous people (as we have seen) and thousands whose names we will never know, from villages, cities, barrios; priests, lay people, women, children, men. The blood of thousands of them is on US hands, because of the part the nation has played in supplying munitions and arms and training to those who kill. The martyrs, while unknown to us, are heartbreakingly known to their wives and fathers and husbands and mothers and grandparents.

Their deaths are celebrated in sorrow but also in hope. When there has been the massacre of a family, or the burning of a village, or a "visit" by a death squad, or an ambush of coffee pickers, or an attack on a child care centre, the people gather, when it is safe to do so, for a memorial service. The names of those attending are read out one by one, and each responds *¡Presente!* (I am here!) And then the names of the murdered victims are read out one by one, and after each name, the people with one voice respond for them: *¡Presente!*

Raphael, killed by a land mine . . . *¡Presente!*
María, machine-gunned in the child care centre . . . *¡Presente!*
Juan, shot defending the hospital . . . *¡Presente!*
José, killed by a sniper . . . *¡Presente!*

Meaning: "He is here . . . she is here . . . they are here . . . *in us*. We speak for them, since they can no longer speak for themselves. We take on their tasks, we will stand where they stood. Teresa will be at the child care centre, Pedro will help defend the hospital. If necessary we will fall as they fell, and if we do, then our names will be read out at another service, and the rest of you will say *¡Presente!* for us, and the struggle will go on until no more guns have to be fired, and we are free."

Sometimes the roll call is even more extensive:

Archbishop Romero . . . *¡Presente!*
Ita Ford . . . *¡Presente!*
Victor Jara . . . *¡Presente!*
Camilo Torres . . . *¡Presente!*

And a prayer will be offered: "Lord, keep alive in us the subversive memory of the martyrs from our people. Let them live in us, and we in them."

Political, or the communion of saints?

No separation.

At the height of the "unrest" on the campuses during the Vietnam war, the chaplain of Yale University, William Sloane Coffin, Jr, was indicted by a federal grand jury for "aiding, counselling, and abetting" young men who felt that they could not fight in a war they perceived as immoral.

This was the last straw for certain red-blooded sons of Eli Yale, who felt it was not the job of "a minister of religion" to be opposing the policies of his government, running around the country "agitating", "fomenting unrest", and counselling others "to break the law". Realizing that Coffin was up for reappointment, the alumni organized a campaign to bring sufficient discredit on him so that no reappointment would be forthcoming. They hoped, by extensive interviewing, to show that Coffin had become so deeply involved in "secular" matters elsewhere that he was failing to mind the "religious" store at home.

The results of their not-so-impartial survey, however, came up with such a different profile of Coffin's activities that the movement to deny him reappointment collapsed. He was, to be sure, "running around the country", speaking, marching, occasionally getting arrested. But a look at Coffin's calendar showed that he was equally busy, if not more so, doing such things as conducting weddings and funerals, preaching the gospel, leading Bible study classes, visiting the sick in the university infirmary, baptizing the children of Yale faculty and students, presiding at the Lord's table on communion Sunday, putting in many hours of counselling each week on a myriad of topics besides Vietnam, praying in public (and presumably also in private), and sharing in panel discussions on everything from sex education to Christian-Jewish relations.

Had he been asked how he kept these two sides of his life together, Coffin would have responded (with an appropriate *bon mot*) that that was the wrong question. There were not "two sides". People worrying about Vietnam have babies and want them baptized; the morality or immorality of public policy is a fit subject for prophetic preaching; making personal decisions about the future can be aided by Bible study; turning points in people's lives often lead them to private prayer and public worship; a student about to turn in his draft card may wish to receive Holy Communion. "If we spend years trying to educate young people to use their consciences," Bill Coffin had long ago decided, "we may not desert them in their hour of conscience."

All of a piece, all of a peace.

During the controversy over apartheid at the University of California at Berkeley in the spring of 1985, a massive rally was held at Sproul Plaza, at which six or seven thousand students gathered to demand that the university divest its holdings in companies doing business in South Africa. The nine theological seminaries up the hill from the university ("Holy Hill", as it is called locally, with varying inflections of affection or disdain) were invited to participate by marching down to Sproul Plaza dressed in ecclesiastical vestments, to give visible witness to the presence and support of the church. Since so many churchy types were to be present, the leaders of the rally decided to depart from custom and begin this particular rally with a prayer, and since I taught at one of the seminaries, I was invited to deliver it.

I worked long and hard on a text that could be delivered over a PA system within the allotted three minutes. (There is a theory on many university campuses that God is either hard of hearing or has a short attention span – and another more credible theory that even if the divine attention span is enduring, the human attention span is pretty short. "Three minutes at most" was the instruction.) When it was time for the rally to begin I was on the podium as instructed, but the legions of the Lord's anointed had not yet put in an appearance, apparently inflicted with the same penchant for tardiness they so deplore when their lay constituencies practise it on Sunday morning.

There was nothing for it but to begin without them, hoping that their late arrival would not be interpreted as lack of commitment. I was scarcely well launched into my plea to the Almighty when there began to be interruptions from the crowd, with a significant enough decibel rating to make me wonder if public prayer at a rally was being looked upon with disfavour by the overwhelmingly "secular" crowd. But the scattered interruptions soon coalesced into a roar – a mighty cheer that made any attempt on my part to continue a futile gesture at best and an arrogant action at worst. I stopped and looked up, intending to wait for silence to be restored, so that I could continue to offer God my carefully crafted prose – and saw a line of hundreds of seminarians, dazzlingly bedecked with their tokens of office (the Episcopalians always come off best), spilling into the crowd, which was acknowledging their arrival with shouts of approval. Their cries, while not the biblical "Hallelujah!" were an adequate modern rendering of that word: "Right *on!*"

As the noise subsided and I prepared to return to my

utterance, it was given to me (in one of those rare visitations of the guiding hand of providence) to realize that I not only need not complete my prayer but that I should not do so. It had already been completed by the action of my colleagues, the solidarity of whose physical presence was spelling out, better than words could ever do, their commitment to this particular issue. *Their deed was their prayer.* They were praying, as was Heschel at Selma, with their feet.

The deed, we are told, authenticates the word. Sometimes, as on this occasion, the deed *becomes* the word.

Elizabeth O'Connor exercises a variety of ministries.

She had been on the staff of the Church of the Saviour, in Washington, DC, since 1953; she has been a "spiritual director" to thousands of people; she occasionally teaches and leads workshops; and she writes penetratingly about prayer, meditation, Bible study and the uses of silence. Presently she is involved in the creation of Sarah's Circle, a ministry to and with the inner-city elderly poor. She is, in sum, a kind of Protestant Henri Nouwen – a comparison that honours them both, as long as we add immediately that Henri Nouwen is a kind of Catholic Elizabeth O'Connor.

Elizabeth O'Connor then, guides people on what she and members of the Church of the Saviour call "the journey inward". But that is not a sufficient description. What makes her contribution so special is her realization that there must simultaneously be a "journey outward", always in company with others. Neither journey alone is sufficient for church or individual.

> While it is a crucial mistake to assume that churches can be on an outward journey without being on an inward one, it is equally disastrous to assume that one can make the journey inward without taking the journey outward. (O'Connor, *Journey Inward, Journey Outward*, p. 9)

So when one joins the Church of the Saviour, in addition to the inner disciplines of engagement with self, God and neighbour there is a "fourth discipline": to become part of a "mission group" and work on a specific project – outreach into the halls of Congress, helping to run a coffeehouse, giving support to a health care centre, focusing on "health advocacy for the poor, empowering the powerless to care and to seek care for themselves".

A brochure describing Wellspring, the church's retreat centre, reminds those going on retreats:

> We share a way of being church that includes two simultaneous journeys – the journey inward and the journey outward. On the inward journey we become more deeply engaged with ourselves, with God, and with others. On the outward journey we join Jesus at a particular point of his ministry to the world, confronting the structures that perpetuate poverty and injustice . . . whatever they may be.

There is a care for balance in dealing with the two journeys, but when the chips are down the priorities are clear. Referring to Meister Eckhart's conviction that it is more important to feed a hungry person than to remain in spiritual ecstasy (a quotation pirated from Elizabeth O'Connor's writings and used in Chapter 8), she continues: "If we had to choose in any given moment between prayer and joining in the struggle of the hungry poor, we would turn from our praying" (O'Connor, *Search for Silence*, p. 118).

Two journeys . . . But since neither can proceed without the other, and both must be undertaken simultaneously, one journey.

The Nicaraguan Minister of State, Miguel d'Escoto, also happens to be a minister of the gospel. As a Catholic priest and member of the order of Maryknoll Missioners he participates in the liturgy which is the Roman mass for many years. He gradually comes to recognize, however, that there is a wider "liturgy" in which he must also participate, the liturgy of working to redeem the social order. And so, leaving the safety of North America where he has lived for several years, he returns to his native land to participate in the people's uprising against a dictator.

After the triumph of the revolution, he accepts appointment to the "secular" position of Minister of State. Along with several other priests he feels called to be both a "minister of God" and a "minister of the people". There is no incompatibility, only complementarity.

The church authorities, however, disagree and discipline Fr d'Escoto and his fellow priests by removing their "faculties": their right to celebrate mass, to hear confession and so on. While this saddens them it does not deter them, and they continue to believe that the "liturgy" to which God calls them includes their work for the state, as the means by which they can best serve the people and thus serve God.

Realizing at one point that options for Nicaraguans and citizens of other countries have been reduced to choosing between various kinds of violence, and believing profoundly in the power of non-violence, Fr d'Escoto does a most unusual thing for a Minister of State. He goes on a public fast for peace, to spark an "evangelical insurrection" and remind the Nicaraguan people and the rest of the world of the need for "a more excellent way". An ancient and usually private liturgical action, fasting is reinvested with meaning as an act of social witness.

The next year, as the Lenten season approaches, Fr d'Escoto goes to the northern border of Nicaragua near Jalapa, target of many US-sponsored terrorist *contra* raids, and begins walking south to Managua, the capital city, re-enacting, with hundreds of Nicaraguans who accompany him, one station of the cross each day of the journey. Fr d'Escoto takes the private journey outdoors and makes it a communal pilgrimage, through which many people can share in Jesus' final struggle and discover new meanings that it might have for them in the future.

These are quite extraordinary happenings, but we will miss the point if we see Fr d'Escoto's religious vision reflected only in fasting and marching, although a religious vision is certainly present in both actions. The really extraordinary thing is the integrity by which he invests the ongoing daily acts of political office with a clear sense that to work for the people in their struggle for social justice is to work for God.

Amen.

Getting onstage ourselves

The author of the Letter to the Hebrews has a final gift for us. After all the action-crammed lines, the extraordinary characters, the frightening and faith-filled episodes about all the folks "back then", she unexpectedly shifts gears. Instead of letting her readers remain on the sidelines, spectators to what is happening on the playing field, she draws the readers out on to the playing field themselves, or (to put it differently), she draws them into the story.

"Therefore," she writes at the end of her historical recital, pausing to catch her breath, therefore . . . but she does not go on, "let us be glad that so many of them ran the race so well." No, the words after "Therefore" are, "since *we* are surrounded by so great a cloud of witnesses . . . let *us* run with perseverance the race that is set before *us*" (Heb. 12:1, italics added).

A little later, saying, "Consider [Jesus] who endured from sinners such hostility against himself", she does not interpolate, "How proud his parents must have been!" No, she writes, "Consider him who endured from sinners such hostility against himself, *so that you may not grow weary or faint-hearted*" (Heb. 12:3, italics added). The story does not end back there. The writer informs us that we are now in the story ourselves. It is no longer only *their* story, it is also *our* story. Welcome onstage.

The deeds that proclaim spirituality/liberation, liberation/spirituality, praxis, shalom – whatever – are not there just to be admired. They are there as signs and pointers to us. This is the way to come, they are telling us. You can't just watch from the sidelines. You have to come onstage. You are part of a community now. You have to venture, to risk. You are needed. After all, the life you save may be someone else's.

An Eccentric Bibliography

"Eccentric" does not necessarily mean strange. It means off centre, a little off track, headed in slightly unexpected directions.

The brief bibliography that follows *is* a little off centre. It is not carefully balanced. Any attempt to catalogue the significant literature on spirituality or liberation with something like equal time for each would soon outstrip the confines of this or any other volume. So what most of the works cited below have in common is that they are attempts, from an initially "liberation" perspective, to develop an understanding that is inclusive of "spirituality" as well. Many come from the third world, which is appropriate at a time when most of us need to begin by listening.

Latin America

Avila, Rafael. *Worship and Politics*. Tr. by Alan Neely. Maryknoll, NY: Orbis Books, 1981.

Betto, Frei. *Fidel and Religion*. Sydney, Australia: Pathfinder Press, 1986.

Boff, Leonardo. *The Lord's Prayer: the prayer of integral liberation*. Tr. Theodore Morrow. Maryknoll, NY, Orbis Books, 1983.

——. *Saint Francis: a model for human liberation*, SCM Press, 1985.

——. *Way of the Cross – Way of Justice*. Tr. John Drury. Maryknoll, NY, Orbis Books, 1980.

Cabestrero, Teófilo. *Ministers of God, Ministers of the People: testimonies of faith from Nicaragua*. Tr. Robert T. Barr. Zed books, 1984.

——. *Mystic of Liberation: a portrait of Bishop Pedro Casaldaliga of Brazil*. Tr. Donald D. Walsh. Maryknoll, NY, Orbis Books, 1981.

Câmara, Helder. *The Desert is Fertile*. Tr. Francis McDonagh. Sheed and Ward, 1976.

Cardenal, Ernesto. *The Gospel in Solentiname*. 4 vols. Tr. Donald D. Walsh. Maryknoll, NY, Orbis Books, 1976–82.

Challenge of Basic Christian Communities. *See* International Ecumenical Congress of Theology.

Fabella, Virginia, and Sergio Torres, eds. *Irruption of the Third World: challenge to theology*. Maryknoll, NY, Orbis Books, 1983; esp. Elsa Tamez *et al*., "Worship service: this hour of history," pp. 181–7.

Galilea, Segundo. *The Beatitudes: to evangelize as Jesus did*. Tr. Robert R. Barr. Gill and Macmillan.

——. *Following Jesus*. Tr. Helen Phillips. Maryknoll, NY, Orbis Books, 1981.

——. "Liberation as an encounter with politics and contemplation". In Claude Geffré, *The Mystical and Political Dimension of the Christian Faith*, pp. 19–33. New York, Seabury Press, 1974.

Gutiérrez, Gustavo. *On Job: God-talk and the suffering of the innocent*. Maryknoll, NY, Orbis Books, 1987.

——. *A Theology of Liberation: history, politics, and salvation*. Tr. and ed. Sister Caridad Inda and John Eagleson. SCM Press.

——. *We Drink from Our Own Wells: the spiritual journey of a people*. Tr. Matthew J. O'Connell. SCM Press.

International Ecumenical Congress of Theology. *The Challenge of Basic Christian Communities*. Papers from the Congress, Feb. 20–Mar. 2, 1980. Ed. Sergio Torres and John Eagleson. Tr. John Drury. Maryknoll, NY, Orbis Books, 1981; esp. Gutiérrez, "The irruption of the poor in Latin America and the Christian communities of the common people," pp. 107–23; Meesters, "The use of the Bible in the Christian communities of the common people," pp. 197–210; "Worship," pp. 217–27; and "Final document," pp. 231–49.

Libañio, J. B. *Spiritual Discernment and Politics: guidelines for religious communities*. Tr. Theodore Morrow. Maryknoll, NY, Orbis Books, 1982.

Nouwen, Henri. *¡Gracias! A Latin American Journal*. San Francisco, Harper & Row, 1983.

Pironio, Eduardo, *et al. Liberación: Diálogos en el CELAM*. Bogotá, CELAM, 1974; esp. "Sentido caminos y espiritualidad de la liberación," pp. 17–25.

Segundo, Juan Luis. *The Hidden Motives of Pastoral Action: Latin American reflections*. Tr. John Drury. Maryknoll, NY, Orbis Books, 1979.

——. *A Theology for Artisans of a New Humanity*. 5 vols. Tr. John Drury. Maryknoll, NY, Orbis Books, 1973–4, esp. vol. 2, *Grace and the Human Condition*, and vol. 4, *The Sacraments Today*.

Sobrino, Jon. *Christology at the Crossroads: a Latin American approach*. Tr. John Drury. Maryknoll, NY, Orbis Books, 1978.

Elsewhere

Balasuriya, Tissa. *The Eucharist and Human Liberation*. Maryknoll, NY, Orbis Books, 1979.

——. *Planetary Theology*. Maryknoll, NY, Orbis Books, 1984.

Brueggemann, Walter, Sharon Parks and Thomas H. Groome. *To Act Justly, Love Tenderly, Walk Humbly: an agenda for ministers*. New York, Paulist Press, 1986.

Carmody, John. *Holistic Spirituality*. New York, Paulist Press, 1983.

Crosby, Michael H. *Spirituality of the Beatitudes: Matthew's challenge for first world Christians*. Maryknoll, NY, Orbis Books, 1981.

De Gruchy, John W. *Cry Justice: Prayers, Meditations,*

[illegible] *...and Readin[illegible] Sou[illegible] Africa*. Ma[illegible] NY, Orbis Books, [illegible]

Dorr, Donal. *Spirituality and Justice*. Gill and Macmillan.

Grassi, J. A. *Broken Bread and Broken Bodies: the Lord's Supper and world hunger*. Maryknoll, NY, Orbis Books, 1985.

Haight, Roger S. *An Alternative Vision: an interpretation of liberation theology*. New York, Paulist Press, 1985.

Heschel, Abraham. *The Insecurity of Freedom: essays on human existence*. New York, Schocken Books, 1972.

——. *The Prophets*. New York, Harper & Row, 1963.

Kavanaugh, John F. *Following Christ in a Consumer Society: the spirituality of cultural resistance*. Maryknoll, NY, Orbis Books, 1981.

Meehan, Francis Xavier. *A Contemporary Social Spirituality*. Maryknoll, NY, Orbis Books, 1982.

Metz, Johannes B. *Theology of the World*. Tr. William Glen-Doepel. New York, Herder & Herder, 1969.

O'Connor, Elizabeth. *Journey Inward, Journey Outward*. New York, Harper & Row, 1975.

——. *Search for Silence*. Waco, Texas, Word Books, 1972.

Sider, Ronald J. *Rich Christians in an Age of Hunger: a biblical study*. Hodder & Stoughton.

Stringfellow, William. *The Politics of Spirituality*. Philadelphia, Westminster Press, 1984.

Wiesel, Elie. *Four Hasidic Masters and their Struggle against Melancholy*. Notre Dame, Ind., University of Notre Dame Press, 1978.

——. *Souls on Fire*. Penguin Books, 1984.